# It's Not
# MY PROBLEM ...
## Or Is It?

From Nudge to Nonprofit

## BRUCE L. BLUMER

*Do good somewhere!*

**PLATYPUS**
PUBLISHING

ISBN: 978-1-959555-68-1


Thank you to Jennifer Manley Rogers / Catchphrase Publishing Services, for her interest, care, and content editing, and for guiding this book to publication.


All profits from this book will be given to support the school and other ministries of Haiti Alive (*EIN*: 46-4179487)
www.HaitiAlive.org

*To Dr. William and Dr. Nathalie Hyppolite, who have taught me much about perseverance, dreaming big, seeing the world with new eyes, and giving back.*

# CONTENTS

*Each chapter opens with a Haitian proverb full of wisdom and insight.*

Chapter One

# INTRODUCTION TO THE WORLD

There's no hiding one's belly when taking a bath.

*(Nan benyen pa gen kache lonbrit.)*

I walked out to the busy street and saw a small boy sitting in the gutter. He was eating a dish that looked like green muck from an old white saucepan. Even though this memory dates from almost fifty years ago, I can clearly see the boy, the pan, and, more than anything, I remember the overwhelming smell. This has become my most vivid impression of poverty—a scene seared into my memory at the young and impressionable age of 16.

Between my junior and senior year of high school, I was selected to be an exchange student. My thought was, why not go to a country that I probably wouldn't visit otherwise during my lifetime? So, I chose Ghana, located in western Africa. Little did I know that this experience would change me from the core.

I spent three months as an exchange student in Ghana while living with a Ghanaian family and absorbing life in a completely different world. I visited places within Ghana where the children had never seen a white person. People looked vastly different in Ghana than in the almost completely white populated state where I was born and raised.

1

With my Ghanaian family and friends, I walked almost every day to buy food from the market, as we had no refrigeration. We ate fufu, casava, plantain, and stews with snail and goat. Time gathering food at the market broadened my palate and changed my perspective on access to food. In Ghana, it's not uncommon to walk a half mile for water to drink, cook, and bathe. This gave me a new perspective on having access to clean water, something I previously had taken for granted. After months in Africa, it angered me to see sprinklers endlessly watering lawns when I returned home.

Toward the end of my three months in Ghana I contracted malaria. Outside the hospital I saw people who had been waiting in line for hours in the hopes of seeing a doctor. This changed my perspective on access to quality health care. As an act of hospitality, I was brought to the front of the line to receive care, but it was a difficult gift to accept when so many others were waiting and suffering in the hot sun.

After a week of recuperating from malaria, I started to feel better, so I thought I'd try to eat some rice, but I couldn't keep it down for long. I ran to the outhouse and saw that one of the doors was cracked. I shoved the door open and projectile vomited on a little girl. I wonder how long she had nightmares of the big white guy crashing in and dousing her!

## In Ghana I began to see the world differently.

It was challenging to process my experiences in Ghana. At that time, I had never heard of culture shock or seen a different way of life but my own. I was a high school male—not long on absorbing and processing feelings. I returned to my friends and a community that was interested in my experience but they couldn't understand fully. But, from that point on, I do know that because of Ghana I began to see the world differently. I can see now how transformative this experience was to my life. It seems that God led me as a young man to a very different place in order to expand my heart, mind, and perspective.

We live largely insulated in this country. The small town in which I grew up was probably 99 percent white. My dad was a pastor, and during my formative years my parents hosted missionaries from Nigeria, Sierra Leone, Indonesia, India, Zimbabwe, Korea, Liberia, and the United States. These were experiences that helped me begin to see beyond my front porch and fuel my desire to consider people who live in other places.

It's easy for some to dismiss things that happen in other countries. Now, because of my personal experience, when something happens in Ghana I'm not tempted to say, "It's not my problem." There are people I know and care about in Ghana. That means there are probably people worthy of knowing and caring about in Detroit, or Santiago, or El Paso, or Beijing. It's not my problem. . . . Or, is it?

From my early years, something was at work deep inside of me. I found that I had an almost innate desire to help. Over much of my adult life, I've pitched in at soup kitchens, food banks, for Habitat for Humanity and on other building projects, aided with flood relief, and assisted on our Native Indian Reservations.

Once when volunteering at a soup kitchen in Chicago, I saw a man standing by himself. I decided to introduce myself.

"Hello," I said. "My name is Bruce."

"Good to meet you," said the man. "I'm Abraham Lincoln."

"As in President Lincoln?"

"Yes," said the man.

"I apologize," I said. "I didn't recognize you."

Now I was fairly confident that President Lincoln wasn't African American. I was even more confident that our sixteenth president had died. Nevertheless, I had a fascinating conversation with this man about what life was like for a former President. How many of you can say you have had a conversation with Honest Abe?

Yet along the way at each of these volunteer opportunities there have been many difficult and painful conversations. The impact of flooding is among the most challenging. Mucking out basements and discarding mud-desecrated belongings are not only physically demanding but also heartbreaking experiences for the families involved.

I remember one such occasion. I went with a group to Grand Forks, North Dakota, to volunteer after a devastating flood. We showed up at one house to find an elderly woman who was paralyzed by her hopelessness. She was sitting in the midst of pictures, soaked furniture, the smell of mold, and completely frozen as far as what to do next. She wasn't expecting anyone to help, as her family lived far away. We didn't put all of her concerns to rest the day we came to her aid, but we allowed some of her fear to melt away by pulling out carpets and spraying down walls, gently guiding her to what should be thrown away, and providing her a moment of support and relief.

> It's about starting where we are, and yet
> not being content with where we are
> and then deciding to go further.

What I've come to understand is the vast majority of people can't or would rather not travel to a foreign country, outside of vacationing at a resort. Many aren't able, physically, to carry buckets of sludge from a basement after a flood or even to stack cans at a food pantry. Not everyone has grown up with generous and world-minded parents that can model moving beyond the familiar in an effort to help others. It's about starting where we are, and yet not being content with where we are and then deciding to go further.

It's also not productive to feel condemnation about the benefits of living where we live but instead being more aware that such benefits may not exist for others. A friend talked to me about "and" thinking. It's possible to enjoy the endless buffets on a pleasure cruise *and* contribute to organizations that provide meals for hungry families. It's buying a house *and* advocating for programs to care for the people sleeping outside on cold nights. It's buying new clothes *and* donating the extras that are gathering dust in our closets to a local ministry.

Who we really are is like trying to hide our bellies when taking a bath. We're exposed and show our true selves. If your family income is around $100,000—you are among 3 percent of the wealthiest people *in the world*. Let that soak in.

We can help others.

Others need us.

It *is* our problem.

My early experiences in Ghana transformed my mind and heart. Now let me take you on the journey that led me toward a deep connection to Haiti.

# HAITI REFLECTION
## Bruce, Team Member

Today I weep for the people of Haiti.

I weep for a place where people won't eat today.

Where children won't go to school this year.

Where someone will die today because there is no medical care.

Where people will wander, looking for work or for hope or for shade.

Where we could help.

We're worried about $4 gas while a child starves.

We're worried about the stock market while a woman dies in childbirth.

We're worried about higher prices at a restaurant while a family eats mud.

We're worried about road construction detours while someone can't find clean water to drink.

We're worried about the meaningless.

We respond with nickels and dimes.

We watch candidates spend millions to be elected who
don't act on behalf of real need.

We listen to athletes gripe about salaries that equal Haiti's
gross national product.

We waste a yearly Haitian salary at the casino.

We build new houses and take vacations and get the latest
electronics.

While someone won't eat today.

While a child won't go to school.

While someone will wander homeless.

While someone will die today.

Where we could help.

# Chapter Two

# BEGINNING CONNECTIONS TO HAITI

*A dog has four legs, but it walks in only one path.*

*(Chen gen kat pye, men li ka mache nan yon sèl chimen.)*

My first trip to Haiti was in 2002. The pastor of our church asked if I'd like to come along with a team that was forming, to spend two weeks in Haiti. It sounded like a great adventure, so I jumped on board. Our church had a long history of helping in Haiti, a country that has an ongoing list of needs, and our church has tried to respond to some of these needs financially and by sending teams.

## Cap-Haitien

This first project was in the north part of Haiti, near Cap-Haitien, the second largest city in Haiti. There is only one international airport in Port-au-Prince, which is the largest city in the country (see maps in appendix A). There is also just one runway, with the international airport and national airport sharing the same airstrip.

To fly from Port-au-Prince to Cap-Haitien, we loaded into a twelve-seater airplane, and I noticed all the signs were written in Russian. *Great*, I thought, *a plane even the Russians don't want.*

When the propellors started up, the man in front of me called to the pilot—the engine was leaking oil. The pilot took a look and said, "Don't worry, you should have seen it last week." A used Russian plane that was leaking oil—what could go wrong?

Our team stayed in the compound of a Haitian minister. Our worksite was in the village of Quartier-Morin, about ten miles from our compound. The daily trips to our worksite gave me the first-hand view of roads in Haiti. Traveling ten miles took forty-five minutes to an hour each way, bouncing in the back of an open pickup. The side of the road you drive on is usually the one you pick, with the goal of trying to avoid potholes and other vehicles. Intersection rules are simple—the biggest vehicle wins and proceeds first. As we traveled, children waved and shouted, "Blan, blan!" which means *white* or *white person*.

## The Worksite

Our project during this, my first trip to Haiti, was to reroof a church. Working alongside locals, we removed the tin, rebuilt some of the wood structures, fixed many of the church pews, repaired doors, and had time to paint as well. Our lunches were simple, peanut butter sandwiches and fruit, but they were eaten solemnly under the gaze of peering eyes staring at us through the church windows. Many of the onlookers gave us the universally understood sign of rubbing their bellies, indicating they were hungry.

One afternoon, I was walking toward a door in the front of the sanctuary and saw a 4x4 beam fall where I knew there were people. I ran and pushed open the door, and Gary was sitting in a chair with his t-shirt ripped open and a scratch from sternum to belly button. The 4x4 had a protruding nail that grazed him. Another half inch and it would have filleted him open from stem to stern. He was just half an inch from a disaster.

Another day, we were painting outside, and a police officer asked if Max and I would come with him. We walked tentatively to a block building with a holding cell, and he asked if we would sit down. Max and I looked at each other and began to wonder what life would be like in a Haitian jail cell. Seemingly enjoying our tension, the officer finally requested, in broken English, our help in getting a visa to the United States. We said we'd try. Heading back to the project site, we knew securing a visa for this man was more than likely to become a futile effort.

On Sunday, we traveled to several small villages to worship. As I recall, the Haitian pastor had a circuit of ten churches, and he'd rotate two or three churches each week, bringing a message, performing baptisms, and serving Communion. We were actually there on World Communion Sunday, and I vividly remember receiving the elements shoulder to shoulder between a Haitian man and woman. My thought in that moment was, *This is what World Communion Sunday is all about.*

The day before our return to the United States, we were able to make phone calls home. Later I found out the 10-minute call to my wife cost about $110. It was the best money I had spent in a long time—I needed that lifeline to home. There was so much to process, so many stories, so many experiences, and needed that connection to the familiar.

One thing that struck me was that although we probably accomplished more than any other team I have been on to Haiti, we lacked connection to the Haitian people. We were secluded in our compound and were tired at the end of the day. But I didn't spend time getting to know the people; my focus was on completing the projects. I knew I had missed out on something this trip.

---

## This country and the people ingrained themselves within my soul.

---

Even though these events and stories happened over twenty years ago, it's as if they happened last week. This country and the people ingrained themselves within my soul and, while I didn't know it at the time, have come to consume much of my time, focus, and heart over the years.

## LaGonave

My second trip to Haiti was in 2008, to the island of LaGonave, a 40 x 10 mile island located in the bay northwest of Port-au-Prince. Upon my return from this trip, my wife said I was a different person (see map in appendix A).

LaGonave is not easy to get to. It's an hour drive north of Port-au-Prince to a boat dock area. Then the options are to take a ferry (with twice as many people as should be allowed, alongside goats, chickens, and bags of charcoal); the Jesus Boat (my name for boats that remind me of those that Jesus and his disciples used, old wooden boats with torn sails, but generally full of people, goats, chickens and charcoal); flyboats (speedboats with two or three engines that sometimes work and, you guessed it, carrying too many people and the extras as previously mentioned); or you can fly in a small plane that lands on a sand and gravel runway, after they shoo the goats and kids off the landing strip.

Although it's challenging to get there, when I arrive on the island of LaGonave, I feel like I'm exactly where I should be. In many ways it is so different than the United States. But LaGonave is rural, laidback, the people are friendly, and it feels like *home*.

On this trip, our project was to support the building of a church. During this effort, we stayed in the Methodist Compound, which contained a church and school. The front wall of the church was crumbling, so that wall was rebuilt, and we started pouring the concrete beams for a future balcony in the church. Concrete in Haiti is mixed on the ground with shovels and carried bucket by bucket to be dropped into forms.

At night we slept in hot, dusty rooms. The house where we slept was on a blind corner for motorcycles, and we heard their horns blaring incessantly. Our outhouse was an adventure at night. We shined our flashlights to encourage the rats and tarantulas to skitter out of our way before entering. The kids came every night to play soccer and to feel our white arms and legs, strange looking to them, and giggle. We witnessed how hungry people care for each other. When we would give out granola bars or candy, these items were generously shared with friends before eaten. We listened to people argue and laugh in a language we couldn't understand. This was the beginning of my connection to and love for the people of LaGonave.

While we were there, missionaries Joe and Shirley Edgerton, who were living and working on LaGonave, asked for a meeting.

They introduced us to a scrawny orphan kid named William. He had a dream to become a doctor. In Haiti, orphans dream to stay alive or for safety or for food, but this one kid had a bigger dream.

William never knew his dad and his mom died when he was about twelve years old. His two sisters were sent to relatives on the mainland while William was sent to LaGonave to live with his uncle, the pastor of the church we were building.

Joe and Shirley asked us to consider sponsoring William to attend medical school. I will never forget that night. We stood in the middle of the church with no roof, under the splendor of the stars, and prayed for a way to support William. We returned to our church back in the States, told them William's story, and the people responded. William began medical school in Port-au-Prince in 2009 because God found a way.

But 2010 began shaky, very shaky.

## HAITI REFLECTION
### Michael—Team Member

Two of us ride in the bed of the pick-up that creeps slowly over ruts and around deep chuckholes, struggling through heavy traffic in the Fort Michel shanty district of Haiti's north coast city, Cap-Haitien. The street is crowded as people pick their way past the goats and shoats and chickens that forage for edible garbage among discarded plastics that lie in the alleys and clog drainage channels and roadside ditches.

Subterranean fires smolder in the landfill on the beach north of Cap-Haitien's pier, releasing dark smoke that curls skyward against the backdrop of the bay and blue Caribbean sky. Stench from burning garbage mingles with heavy exhaust fumes spewed by rusted cars and battered trucks. Worn engine valves mean good business for street vendors selling quarts of motor oil here and there along the main road.

Grimy from a day of hard work in high humidity and heat, coughing in the road dust and exhaust fumes, we are returning to an abandoned guest house where we are barracked for two weeks while working on a construction project sponsored by our Methodist Church back home.

Each day after work, as we inch homeward through traffic, many brightly painted "tap-tap" trucks that normally carry people around the city begin to empty out. Pedestrians can proceed faster right now than any vehicle. People sidestep vendors, skirt garbage heaps, dodge around abandoned car frames that have been completely stripped of anything useful.

Makeshift homes of cement block, concrete, battered wood sheeting, and corrugated tin lean together along narrow winding alleys that spiderweb outward from three major roads that intersect in downtown. The alleys are channels for garbage and sewage runoff, and after rain they sluice debris into Cap-Haitien Bay where it bobs heavily in muddy swells coming in from the sea.

Though Cap-Haitien has been our base while here, we are working on the trusses and roof and doors of a Haitian church in the village of Quartier-Morin, about forty-five minutes away. Two of our volunteers, Paul and Tiffany, respectively a dentist and nurse, planned to run a dental clinic, but today they find trouble.

Their car becomes stuck in traffic far behind burning barricades. Not knowing better, with their driver they get out and walk ahead to see what is going on. Paul had been taking pictures and still has his camera around his neck on a strap. Two demonstrators see and point to the camera and scream at him.. Bottles come flying over the barricade and shatter in front of them. They are chased a short distance but make it back to their car, unharmed but badly shaken. Their driver maneuvers out of the traffic blockage and, reversing direction, drives away from the scene. Although only a couple of miles from the compound, they spend the next four hours threading their way around flooded areas before they arrive safely back to tell us their story.

Raining or not, brown water drips through the ceiling of the room where we eat our meals, and we periodically empty the basin we place on the floor to catch the water. The plumbing does not work so we haul water buckets filled at an outside cistern to our bathroom on the second floor. Taking numerous trips up and down stairs, we fill a fifty-gallon barrel, then treat the water with a bit of bleach.

We take turns bathing in the evening: stand in rusty bath-
tub; fill big sauce pan with water from barrel; pour water
over head; soap up and scrub; repeat with kettles of rinse
water. Haul more water to fill toilet tank so can flush toilet
after several of us have used it. And so forth.

Near our guest house in Cap Haitien, the first sun-
light pokes above the horizon and the bay blooms bril-
liant orange. Small dory boats in black silhouette move
north from Fort Michel, putting out their nets. One man
rows and another passes netting over the stern, each in
synchrony with the other. The oars, the men, the boats,
the nets: all lift and plunge rhythmically through the slow
swells. As one boat passes, I hear the men talking, the
cadenced "thunk" of oars in their locks, the "whoosh' of
netting as it streams into the water. Another Creole saying: "God is good."

At our work project, I take a break from ripping off
rusted corrugated roofing and climb down to help our
nurse, Tiffany. She is treating numerous children with
open sores on their arms and legs. Each of these pin
worm sites are surrounded by ants and other bugs that
drink from the open wounds. We brush the bugs away
and apply hydrogen peroxide, antibiotic ointment, and
band-aids. Old scar tissue that surrounds the active sores
on most kids' legs betray the presence of chronic worm
infestations. Our treatments are merely cosmetic, but
each kid is mesmerized, thrilled at the careful attention

we give to each of them. Tiffany tells me that cheap worm medicine would easily solve these issues, but none reaches Quartier-Morin.

Several older men and women stop to watch or help us through the days as we tear off rusty tin, rebuild trusses, and reinstall new tin. A toothless old man works with us one day. He appears in torn khaki shorts and a faded purple (and much too big) wool cardigan sweater with the sleeves rolled up, though they still fall to his wrists. Deeply stooped, his bare feet like elephant hide, he smiles continuously but never speaks. He seems to know what needs to be done before we ourselves know. After that day we never see him again.

One face haunts me. Several times over a period of days, a lady visits us. Her hair is always matted and unwashed, done up in a few tangled pigtails. She wears the same dirty dress each day and carries a rickety folding chair. She never speaks but sits close in front of the church and silently watches through a brick grating as we paint the interior walls. Always somber and affectless, perhaps she suffers from depression or some other ill. She is quite alone amid our chaotic work scene full of whirling school kids and hammering. One day, perhaps having seen enough, she departs and never comes back. So many people in the world, so many anonymous, lonely souls.

We wind our way past the open charcoal market from which people depart with huge bags of cooking charcoal hoisted onto their shoulders. For blocks in all directions, the soot of charcoal dust covers the ground. A truck driver holds a loudspeaker and delivers a political harangue in Creole, but no one gives a show of listening. Ahead of us car horns blare in frustration at an unseen bottleneck somewhere around the curve toward Rue 3.

A man in torn pants and sleeveless tee-shirt wields a machete, chopping and sawing at a fly-swarmed side of beef that hangs from a spike on a utility pole. A massive tangle of bootleg wiring above him on the pole leads off in dozens of directions toward surrounding buildings. A dog with mangy flanks licks at a bloody puddle at the man's feet, until he jabs at it with the tip of his machete. The dog retreats a couple of steps, and the man goes back to work on the carcass. The dog slinks forward to the puddle and begins to drink again.

Another man in a sweat-stained Cincinnati Reds baseball cap drives four head of emaciated cattle down the road, each of them tethered to him by long frayed ropes. Two of the animals carry woven vine baskets full of oranges, bananas, and mangoes. He is headed toward the open market at Fort Michel. Periodically, he taps them with a long, willowy branch. For a few seconds they pick up the pace, then drop back to a slow plod once more.

Women are everywhere on the road going to and from the market. Towels are wrapped tightly around their heads to cushion and support their loads: plastic or metal wash basins with bulk rice, bananas, chicken parts, man-goes, utensils, laundry. Sometimes these loads are stacked two or three baskets high, adding dramatically to each woman's height.

A day or two later our work is finished. We pack up everything and ready ourselves to leave the job site. A few children, both boys and girls, during our time there have asked me and others: "Would you be my father?" Few if any of them speak English at their age, so someone else has helped them memorize that question. Such a plea is quite hard to hear, thinking of all the pain that lies behind it. How to help a sorrowful child, or the larger world stricken with an unhealable wound that goes right to the heart of this life.

On the way to the airport in the morning, we pass a brightly painted tap-tap with only one passenger, an old man holding two chickens in his lap. The chickens look dazed, as if resigned to their fate. Red letters on the back of the tap-tap canopy read, "Repent! All of you!"

Sound advice for the entire world, too rarely taken.

The obvious thought gnaws at me: We have spent two weeks in Haiti, but never settling in more than skin deep, never in the game or even near it. We are well intentioned volunteers, clutching our passports and return tickets tightly, we fly home to our snug firesides and tell our tales.

Chapter Three

# THE EARTHQUAKE

The rock in the water does not know
the pain of the rock in the sun.

*(Woch nan dio pa konnen doulewoch nan soley.)*

My third trip to Haiti was a trip that almost didn't happen. There was a terrible snowstorm and many of the roads across the state were closed. Our team of twelve members was leaving from western South Dakota, so my son and I had to drive there by going north and busting through drifts on secondary roads until the interstate reopened. Then our flights were cancelled, but a wonderful man rearranged our schedules so, finally, we could arrive in Haiti. I remember making it to our site on LaGonave and thinking, *It's going to be a breeze from here.* Famous last words!

Our team arrived on a Sunday and set up a clinic at the Celebrate Jesus compound where droves of people came seeking medical care. People waited in the pews of the church to be seen by our medical staff. I remember walking by the church the following day, a Monday. So many people waited all day and would come back the next day and wait *again* before receiving care. . . . Then on Tuesday the earthquake hit.

## Earthquake Day

Tuesday, January 12, 2010, 4:53 p.m. While I was walking toward our pharmacy inside the clinic I heard a rumble. It sounded like kids running on the stairs, but that couldn't be. Then it sounded like a train, and that surely couldn't be—no trains in Haiti. Then the ground simply moved and it was disorienting. People ran out to the open field and waited. Some of our team were sick to their stomachs from the movement. We joked, "Hey, cool, we've just been through our first earthquake." After we went back into the clinic there was a major aftershock. It was decided—no more clinic that day. Luckily, a doctor on our team got a quick phone call out to his wife that we were OK. That was the last direct communication we'd have for several days.

We actually didn't know what had happened in the capital of Port-au-Prince. We were only about twenty-five miles from the epicenter of the earthquake, but LaGonave is rural with no tall buildings and few people. The night of the earthquake, the organizers didn't want us to sleep in the building, so we brought our mattresses into the open field. The hillside looked like it had snowed—there were several hundred people sleeping on sheets across the field who were too afraid to be inside their homes, as there were many aftershocks that night and in the days to come.

Later the next day my son went to the center of the town to connect with the Wesleyan Compound and get information. When he returned, the look on his face told it all. "It's bad, Dad."

We began to hear from others that this was a major catastrophe. In Haiti when people find out about a death, there is a bellowing cry. We heard too many of these over the next few days. That night there was a worship service in the church and the people were singing and praying. A voodoo group came up the path and began drumming and chanting loudly during our worship. The church group began praying and singing louder. The drumming/chanting and the praying/singing kept escalating. It seemed like a contest—"Whose God is stronger?"

My son continued to go daily to the town, to try to send email messages. We weren't in any immediate danger. We had food and water. It just wasn't clear how we were going to get home. Our clinic was located on a highpoint, and we had a flat area off the second floor where we could sit. From this vantage point we could see ships and planes arriving that we later learned were providing relief assistance.

On Thursday we started to receive people from Port-au-Prince who were injured. This was astonishing, because LaGonave is an hour trip north of the city, a boat ride through the bay, and then our clinic was a bumpy thirty- to forty-five-minute trip up the hill. Yet somehow, these patients in need reached us. People came with lacerations, a broken hip, and many broken bones. One woman arrived who had burns on her abdomen and legs from cooking oil. The doctors said if she had been in the United States she would have been transferred immediately to a burn center. Too much trauma overran our little clinic to respond effectively. We sent word that we were closing our clinic, and we hauled all our medicine and supplies to one hospital on the little island and we waited.

A few days after the earthquake, I woke early. The bay was bathed in the beautiful colors of dawn. A lone sailboat was gliding along the shore. This image was tempered with the reality that across the serene water, thousands of people had died, and many more thousands were displaced and had uncertain futures. It made me realize, like the tragedy far across the bay, despite how things look especially from a distance, we never really know what's going on in other peoples' lives.

---

## We never really know what's going on in other people's lives.

---

During the initial days after the earthquake, it was much harder on our families back home than for us. They were seeing terrible images in the media of death and destruction in Port-au-Prince and, at first, we didn't even know the extent of what had happened. My wife and my parents were stunned and numb. Later, hearing stories from families of the team regarding those days before we could share we were OK broke our hearts—we were fine; we just had no way to communicate promptly with our loved ones after the earthquake hit.

While we were waiting to find out our next steps, an interpreter stopped by and wanted to talk to our team. He said that if we ran low on food, he would bring some from his home. His own ability to get food would be diminished, now that Port-au-Prince was in disarray, and we had more food in our kitchen than this man and his family would eat in two months. Yet he offered us a gift—a gift beyond measure.

---

## He offered us a gift—a gift beyond measure.

---

The Wesleyan Compound, who we were staying in communication with, sent a message for me to come; they had a way for us to get off the island. First, they were rescuing fifteen youth from another area and bringing them to combine with our team as well as others on LaGonave. We would all travel across the bay in a lobster boat. Then, most would go north by truck and have a very bumpy, dusty, dirty ride and leave from a cargo plane from Cap-Haitien. The remaining ten of us would go into Port-au-Prince and leave from a private *Amway* jet that was delivering doctors and medical supplies (see map in appendix A).

When we brought the medicines to the hospital, I had included my medications for diverticulitis. Probably due to the stress, I started having symptoms. I began to wonder if they would put on my tombstone, "He gave his medicines away." We stopped by the hospital to beg for my medicines to be returned, which they graciously did. I also felt guilt for sending two members of the team to the north when I was set to go home on a private jet.

## HAITI REFLECTION
### Sarah—Team Member, Medical Provider

A few days after the earthquake, we knew we had gone from being in service to our Haitian friends to being more of a burden. Although I am a nurse practitioner, I remember feeling helpless. We had decided to donate all our remaining medications and supplies and closed our clinic.

I don't remember now how I got to the hospital, but it was eerily quiet. The halls were empty, the rooms looked like they had been stripped. The patients were outside in the courtyard lying on mattresses on the ground because everyone was afraid that the hospital would collapse with the aftershocks. People had erected makeshift tent shelters over their family members to keep the sun off them. They were so afraid.

The helpless feeling continued as I wandered down the silent, cracked hallways, looking for someone to talk to. Many of the doctors had left for Port-au-Prince to help in hospitals there, where the damage was unbelievable.

I heard voices and someone crying out. I peered through a small window and into the dim operating room. There was no electricity. I saw a pregnant woman lying on the operating table. She was awake and calling out over and over "Jesu, Jesu, Jesu."

A nurse held her hand. There was no anesthesiologist. I could not look away as I watched the physician do a cesarean, using only local anesthetic, to deliver her overdue baby. I helped in the only way I could; I stood as a witness and prayed.

Her last baby was still-born at forty-two weeks, the physician told me. Part of a different medical mission team, he said he was glad to be in the right place at the right time, to help bring a healthy baby into the world in the midst of chaos.

## The Experience in Port-au-Prince

The ride through Port-au-Prince was staggering. Five story buildings had pancaked into one story buildings. Rubble and fires were everywhere. The smell of death and hopelessness lingered in the air. We'd had a much different experience than those who went through the earthquake and aftermath in Port-au-Prince and the surrounding area.

When we arrived at the place where we would spend the night, the men were given an outbuilding where we would sleep. One of the older team members became annoyed with the flies. He demanded that I go find a fly swatter. He continued to be more and more demanding. I went inside and asked, "I know the answer, but do you have a flyswatter?" And I brought back the answer he didn't want to hear. In retrospect, I realized that a sense of control over simple things is cherished when so much is out of your control.

We arrived at the airport the following morning and there were hordes of people trying to find a way out of the country. The Haitian guards asked if I had the tail number of the plane that was coming for us. When I didn't have that number, he said we would not be allowed in. In a demanding voice I said, "Send someone from the United States." A few minutes later, Officer Rodriguez appeared at the door in his full army fatigues and an automatic weapon strapped across his chest. I explained we had an *Amway* jet coming, we didn't have the tail number because we've had almost no access to technology, and we needed to get into the airport. He said, "Follow me." We walked through a fractured terminal to a waiting area alongside the landing strip.

The relief effort, even in the early days, was incredible. We saw planes and supplies that were being flown in from around the world—Spain, Canada, Argentina, England, the United States, and so many other places. Logistics were difficult, to say the least. There is ONE runway in Port-au-Prince, so getting airplanes in and out was a nightmare. There is one main gate to leave the airport, the only place for supplies to get out. Throngs of people were waiting at the gate in hopes of receiving food, water, or other supplies that had been flown into the country. I walked with the *Amway* team leader to show him the gate, and I asked a military person what was going on. He said that it was getting dangerous with too many people pressing in around the gate. This meant they would have to close the only gate until they could get the situation under control. The leader said, "Get on the plane, we'll figure it out." The logistics in Haiti are difficult in the best of times and these were not the best of times.

In spite of the challenges, we had it much easier than so many others. Our friends and missionaries, Joe and Shirley Edgerton, had to identify and bring the body of Rev. Sam Dixon back to the States. Joe and Shirley made a last-minute decision not to have lunch with Sam and others, a decision that could have changed, if not ended, their lives. We didn't have to deal with broken bodies and lost lives and confusion and pain on a magnitude greater than the earthquake.

A few months after the earthquake I was sitting in my car at a traffic light. A concrete truck rumbled up alongside me, and the vibration and noise gave me a startle. I remember slapping my hands down on the seat with a moment of panic. Like many that go through a difficult situation, the memories are below the surface but not that far below.

William had started medical school in Port-au-Prince but was with our medical team during the earthquake. This was a fortunate thing, as his medical school collapsed and many of his instructors and fellow students were killed. William came up with a new plan, to start medical school in the Dominican Republic. He set off for a place where he had no place to live, where they would accept none of his Haiti medical school classes, and he was going to have to learn a new language—Spanish. Our church and supporters responded again. William and two friends headed to a new adventure; his school and living costs were covered for the next five years.

In addition to supporting William's medical school and living costs, funds raised were used to support other students with tuition costs, supply needed medicine for mobile clinics, provide food for the elderly, and help with other small projects.

We are rocks in the water, not fully understanding the pain of the rocks in the sun. My dad told me recently that when he heard from or looked at the group who was there during the earthquake, most came back and said, never again. "But you came back," he said, "and you said, 'I need to do something.'"

Chapter Four

# CONNECTIONS TO LAGONAVE

What you do is what you see.

*(Sa ou fe, se li ou we.)*

After recovering from the earthquake experience, I felt an urge to get back to the island of LaGonave. I also knew that once there, it would be time to listen, not talk. We tend to be fixers and bring our well-intentioned ideas that we impose on those who are living in extremely different circumstances that we know little about.

In 2011 I went to Haiti by myself. I arranged to visit as many leaders, pastors, women's groups, and individuals as I could, asking this simple question, "If we could help, what do you need?"

With an interpreter I traveled to five small villages around the island of LaGonave. We sat under trees with groups of women. We sat with pastors on wood slats nailed to posts sunk in the ground that served as pews for the church. We sat on porches with community leaders. We sat with the elderly under blue tarps, to shade us from the burning sun. We spent long, dusty days traveling to remote places. We listened.

Communicating with an interpreter is always tricky. Although translation is slow and sometimes tedious, you hope that the conveyed message represents the true intent of the words.

What I found was incredibly resilient and hopeful people, people who use limited resources to try to make tomorrow a fraction better. Of the millions of dollars of relief supplies that poured into Haiti after the earthquake, a miniscule amount found its way to LaGonave. The conversations I had on this solo trip reinforced my resolve to do *something*.

---

## These conversations reinforced my resolve to do *something*.

---

The two women's groups I met with opened my eyes to the difficult lives of women and how much they did for their families and communities. Both of the groups were organized to support women, caring for each other as they have a tough path in Haiti.

These groups of women meet regularly and they collect a small amount of dues from each woman. These funds help other women to finance small businesses, often called micro-loans. On one trip to LaGonave my wife taught a basic business class to a group of women. If you buy, let's say, mangoes, you need to sell them for more, repay your original loan, and then use the profits for your family. "But what if my child gets sick? What if we have no food? What if something breaks and it needs to be replaced?" Budgeting is difficult, and it's easy to understand why their businesses sometimes fall short.

They also reach out to sick and suffering women, assist the elderly (especially women), buy clothes for children, and keep them safe from becoming domestics—child slaves. Families in the rural areas will give their child to families in the bigger towns with the promise that their child will be educated and cared for, and it's rare that either of those promises will be delivered.

Haiti is a very male dominated society. While I don't fully understand, the men do little yet want to control everything. We've also found, through our medical teams, that many women don't understand sexual issues. One of the women asked the doctor if she could look inside and see how many babies she had left in there. This was a question asked in the year 2020. This dynamic of dominance and lack of understanding leads to lots of babies. Many women have children from multiple fathers.

One group started a chicken and egg business. They showed me the coop they'd made from woven vines and sticks. They would sell the eggs to support their projects. Unfortunately, something happened to a couple of their hens, which impacted their business.

Access to clean water is an issue across the island of LaGonave. These women know that water means health and life and it was a concern. I ask you to try something—seriously. Get a bucket, any size, fill it with water and walk a mile. It represents what many families do every day. First, you'll find that water is heavy. And then you'll realize that every drop that spills out of your bucket is a drop less to drink, bathe, cook, or clean.

One day I watched a woman getting water from one of the town wells. She'd obviously had a stroke, drug one foot, and could only use one arm. She'd walk a gallon container about 30 feet. Then walk back, pick up the second gallon jug and walk 30 feet past the first container. This repeated itself over and over and over—until she got to the well and then back home.

Many women spoke about their lack of healthcare. These villages are so far from a clinic and even farther from a hospital.

Simple burns or cuts, things which we can care for easily back home, can become life threatening in Haiti.

The leaders of both women's groups were young, intelligent, and had strong resolve. My worry was, will they be able to stay and support women in these small, rural communities? Helping women is definitely going to be on the list.

I met with several pastors and members of their churches. In one church, the earthquake had taken the walls down and they needed a place to worship. One of the churches wanted to start a feeding program for the elderly and an agricultural program so the community could raise some of their own food.

One pastor saw so many children in the street that he began a school for that area. The school is in a part of town that has great needs, but the parents do not have the ability to pay him. His teachers are volunteers at this point, but they hope for a sponsor to pay for supplies and the teachers wages.

There's a church in a village who is reaching young families. These families are donating their time and skills and what little funds they have to build a church and school. The pastor is emphatic that the spiritual needs be met first and serving others after. The church holds classes to teach people life skills and they have a remarkable community outreach considering their limited resources.

Schools are often connected to churches. It was clear that education is a priority for the people and needs to be on our list.

The elderly hold a special place in my heart. Honestly, I'm not sure how you grow old in Haiti. Lack of healthcare, no retirement accounts, no support from the government, and abysmal living conditions face most of our aging friends. I was thinking about the health conditions of my own family, and it's probable that my parents, siblings, and I already would be deceased if we lived in Haiti. We all have had issues that can be cared for successfully in the United States but would likely be fatal in Haiti.

Most of the elders we visited with made their living by way of physical labor. They were planters, cassava grinders, those who cut down trees to make charcoal, brick makers, a woman who washed clothes for others, and some sold small items. For the most part, if you don't work in Haiti, you don't eat. Other than living off the kindness of family and friends, food is a daily question mark that must be answered.

Two themes, from the elderly I interviewed, were repeated to me over and over—a deep faith in God and a life of suffering. They would say things like "God protects me" or "I hold on to God's hand" or "God is the only one that cares for me" while at the same time saying they were sick but couldn't find or afford medical care, it was too dry to grow plants, people could be cruel to them, and they hoped someone would see that they had no fire and would drop off food. Some had family, but those families had problems of their own.

Could I praise God if my life was miserable? Maybe it's the only hope they can count on. Hope for a better life to come, after enduring a hard life on earth. Elderly and healthcare are on the list.

In my travels to these communities, I also discovered the splendor of LaGonave. It's a beautiful, Caribbean island surrounded by a stunning ocean. It may surprise you, but LaGonave has a desert climate. There are cacti and desert flora abounding on the island. When you go "up the mountain" there is better soil, slightly cooler temperatures, and more vegetation. It's there they have larger trees, where they grow coffee, peanuts, and a variety of beans. Clean water comes from mountain springs or directing rainwater into cisterns or catchments. Water is a huge issue for the entire island.

Haiti itself is a mountainous country. Paul Farmer wrote a book entitled *Mountains beyond Mountains*. It's an engaging book about his ministry with Haiti, but it describes the topography well; it's mountains and then there's more mountains. There are large parts of Haiti and LaGonave that are uninhabited and uninhabitable. Unfortunately, the earthquake missed those areas and picked an area with a high concentration of people and buildings.

> I laughed every day. I cried every day. I hoped every day. I prayed every day for a way.

This trip was special. I laughed every day. I cried every day. I hoped every day. I prayed every day for a way. By the end of my travels the themes were so clear—education, healthcare, and how to alleviate the difficulties experienced by women, children, and the elderly. So that's been our focus as a nonprofit from the beginning and remains our focus to this day.

## The Nudge to Do Something

After the earthquake trip, I put together a booklet called *Paths, Proverbs, and Lessons from Haiti*. It contains reflections from those that had been in the earthquake with lots of pictures of people on LaGonave. Individuals back home expressed much interest and truly wanted to help. By going to churches, speaking to groups, and asking for a donation for the booklet, we were able to raise around $20,000. This was an early step on our path. Problems in Haiti became problems we cared about. It may not have been enough, but it was something.

Because our church had a long history of helping in Haiti, it was natural to have people give through the church to support projects and ministries. In prior years, the church supported a "school lunch program," then solar ovens, and the church sponsored several mission teams to LaGonave.

At first, we gave funds to the people that I had connected with on my trip to the villages. We gave small amounts to the women's groups and scholarships for schools, sent funds for medications, and began feeding programs for the elderly. We were running the funds through our local church, which was logical considering their ongoing connection with Haiti. The logistics of getting money to small villages weren't easy or sustainable.

In spite of our best efforts, what we learned was that there is an inherent unfairness about helping. If you buy food for fifty people, what about person number fifty-one, or fifty-two? If you buy medicine for a village, what happens when the medicine runs out and the shelves are bare? If you build a clinic in one area, what about the others? If you financially support a great project initiated by the local women's group, what happens when the next great idea comes along, but there's no money left in the mission account?

I will say this and will repeat it until you believe it—there have been countless times when I've thought or prayed, "God, we are short again!" because we didn't have money for a project. And a check would show up. It's happened way too many times for me to pass it off as a simple coincidence.

Chapter Five

# BEGINNING A NONPROFIT

A horse with ten masters will die tied to its post.

*(Chwal ki gen dis mèt mouri nan poto.)*

Step by step, story by story, donor by donor, our ministry grew. Then the unexpected happened.

One day, the pastor of our church asked if we could meet for coffee. At this meeting, the pastor informed me that the church would no longer be able to receive or distribute donations for the ministry and needs in Haiti.

This was an unexpected conversation. Quickly we needed to find a new way to receive donations. A pastor friend who lived in another state came to mind, so I called him to explain our situation. I asked if donations could be received through his church while we applied for nonprofit status. My friend said his church would be honored to help. So, for a year, we took on the clunky process of sending funds to a different church out of state and then receiving those very funds back to support projects on LaGonave. As a temporary solution, it worked, and it bought us more time to take on and complete the nonprofit application process.

While it didn't seem like it at the moment, these events ultimately worked in our favor. Having our own nonprofit would allow us to engage support more easily from outside the church. While not the intention, working through church committees can be cumbersome and time consuming. By becoming a nonprofit, we are now able to make our own decisions and move more nimbly to meet urgent needs.

Now if you Google Haiti nonprofits, you'll see a multitude of organizations with the word Haiti in their names. But even seasoned travelers to Haiti often don't know that LaGonave exists. I wanted people to know about the needs of this island, so I originally used LaGonave in our nonprofit name.

We became a registered nonprofit in November of 2013, and LaGonave Alive! was born. One of our sons created the logo, and our other son set up the website. Luckily for Haiti, I don't know how to hunt or fish, so LaGonave and the nonprofit became my hobby, and some might even say obsession!

I'm a slow learner. It took me almost ten years to absorb the fact that the original name of our nonprofit, LaGonave Alive, might be a challenge for folks. Going by the name alone, it's difficult to identify the place and nature of the ministry. The name is also hard to pronounce and remember. It sounds like *la – la – la* when you say LaGonave, and so it requires constant spelling out. The week our Board was going to vote on the name change, three members sent me emails in which all three misspelled *LaGonave*. This confirmed we needed to change the name, without a doubt! And so, in 2022, we officially changed the name and logo of our nonprofit to *Haiti Alive*. On all correspondence, our name appears as "Haiti Alive, a LaGonave ministry." For clarity, I will use *Haiti Alive* in the book when referring to our nonprofit, even though we were known as *LaGonave Alive!* for almost ten years.

You may notice that both our logos have a sailboat image (see appendix B). There are always wooden boats with sails in the bay of LaGonave. That image endured for me after the earthquake.

If you're considering becoming a nonprofit, first, I'll say that not every promising idea needs to become a nonprofit organization. If you can work through another entity, that is ideal, as you begin. Look at the registry in your state; you'll be shocked by how many nonprofits there are and how many are involved in work similar to yours. It is also important to remember that until your organization goes through the IRS 501c3 process, donors are not able to count their gifts to you as charitable contributions.

I'll provide an overview of the process of becoming a nonprofit, but my suggestion is to start by finding a sympathetic lawyer and CPA. The firms that applied for us only charged us for application fees. It was a nice gift.

This following information can be found at www.nolo.com.

1. Choose a name. Your name should be unique; check the nonprofit list from your state's secretary of state office to be sure you don't duplicate. It's also a good idea to see if that name is available for a website address.

2. File articles of incorporation. There are model articles of incorporation and these need to be filed with your state office. The www.nolo.com website has links to the guide for each state.

3. Apply for your IRS tax exemption. When articles of incorporation are approved by your state and you become a recognized domestic nonprofit, you will then apply with the IRS. It is an online process but be prepared: the IRS

is slow with processing and it can be a challenge to get customer service responses.

4. Apply for a state tax exemption. This does not apply in all states. In South Dakota, we were accepted as a Domestic Nonprofit and did not need to file a state tax exemption.

5. Draft bylaws. Again, there are model documents. You need to think about who will serve as officers, the number and terms of board members, your annual meeting, replacing and removing officers, and other items regarding how your board will function. We added later to our bylaws that we could meet and take votes electronically as our board members live across a couple states.

6. Appoint directors. My suggestion is to find people who are sympathetic to your ministry but also consider what they can bring to your board—volunteer work, connections, funding, social media/marketing, financial knowledge, and property are just some of the considerations.

7. Hold a meeting of the board. You will need to hold an initial meeting and then annual meetings each year to elect officers. An agenda and minutes need to be created and provided for the board.

8. Obtain licenses and permits. This varies state by state.

   • We have our board sign an annual Conflict of Interest policy. Some organizations have a job description for the board that is signed upon being accepted to the board.

   • We decided to purchase a Board & Directors Liability plan, to protect our board, but there is a cost.

- It is expensive, but we hire a CPA firm to do our 990 filing. Filing the 990 is required to maintain your tax-exempt status, but we decided we wanted an outside review of our finances for accountability.
- We applied for recognition from Guidestar/Candid. It is an online process, but it's a mark of transparency and follows industry standards for nonprofits. Many corporations use this as a guideline for nonprofit giving.

As mentioned, we went through a name change process. It's a slow process. We filed in September, received approval from the IRS in December, and the name change didn't appear on their website until April. We've had some transition issues, mostly with large corporations who look to the IRS website for information. Other than slow processing, it has largely been a smooth transition.

Chapter Six

# FOUR PRINCIPLES OF FUNDRAISING

People talk and don't act. God acts and doesn't talk.

*(Neg di san fe. Bondye fesan di.)*

While I have had multiple jobs, I've basically had two career fields: education for twenty-five years and foundation/ fundraising for eighteen years. I was a teacher and administrator in education from elementary through college, and I was involved in foundation and fundraising for church, school, and nonprofit organizations. Working in these two arenas has given me perspective. Here are my four principles for any nonprofit (and, honestly, your church, school, or business):

**1. Set your mission and focus and make sure they drive your decisions.**

No organization can be all things to all people. The broader your scope the more difficult it is to tell your story and explain to people what you do. Increasingly, donors (and especially younger donors) want targeted giving. They want to see the impact of their gift and may be short-term givers. They will give to a very specific project and the next one may not interest them, so they move on.

Online giving formats often take a fee, but if you are set up to receive donations in this manner, you will receive more gifts that are more "impulse" or "in the moment." Online giving formats allow you to receive donations that you would not normally receive if, for example, you only took checks or if your website requires too many steps to make a donation. Many see a ministry that catches their interest, give, and go.

We started Haiti Alive with three areas of focus: education, healthcare, and supporting women, children, and the elderly. These areas remain our focus today. Over the years we've had people ask if we would support a water project or agriculture development plan or begin a church. All worthy ventures! Unless they are directly supportive of our three areas, we've had to say, "It's needed, it's worthy, but we just can't take on another area of focus."

We are currently building a Women's Village that includes simple homes for women and their children. We are putting bathrooms in the homes, with flush toilets that will go into a septic tank system. These families need water to flush the toilets and clean water to drink. So, we have dug wells in the Village to support these women and children. We believe that supports our core areas, even though the specific component is a water project.

Our ministry has grown but we're still a small nonprofit. We do all we can to support and maintain our current projects. We work to provide donors with stories of impact, so they know what our mission is and how they can focus their giving.

## The Mission of Haiti Alive

*Haiti Alive is a nonprofit organized to serve God and to bring hope, health, and happiness to the people on the island of LaGonave, Haiti. We convey the message of Christ through the areas of education, healthcare, and ministering to those in need, especially women, children, and the elderly.*

Our ministry grew out of a church, and we maintained that religious component when we became a nonprofit. We believe the best way to show God's love is by following the example of Christ, through caring for and supporting the people. While we are rooted in faith, our nonprofit hasn't built a church and we do not force Christianity on our friends. Matthew 25: 34-40 is a verse that guides us. "The King [Jesus] will reply, 'Truly I tell you, whatever you did for one of the least of these brothers and sisters of mine, you did for me'" (Matthew 25: 40 NIV). We follow the principal attributed to Francis of Assisi as well, "Preach the Gospel at all times. If necessary, use words."

Our mission and focus areas are clear, and we consciously let these drive our decisions. As a former educator, Madeline Hunter was popular for a while, and she promoted an instructional design model. She often used the phrase, "Do less, well." That should guide every organization.

## 2. Don't make planning a crutch for inaction. Know where you're headed and go do something.

If you've been connected to a school, church, or organization, you've likely been part of a planning process.

Now I'm not anti-planning, but I do believe that planning can become a crutch for inaction. It's WAY easier to plan and prepare than it is to actually do something. Fear of failure seems to be at the root of it.

An organization that shall remain anonymous has entered its second year of planning, with virtually no change in the way they function. Even if some mistakes will be made, I say, go do something. Even if it's the wrong focus, it will be better than sucking the life out of everyone related to the organization by over planning, and you might accidentally help someone by getting out there. These planning processes look like action, but it's a cover for inaction. It's easier to plan than to do the hard work of actually *doing*.

Plan. Do something. Then adjust and keep doing.

A hungry donkey finds himself between two equally large and delicious-looking bales of hay. He looks from one to the other and back again, unsure which to choose. This goes on for a long while until, unable to make a decision, the poor old donkey dies of starvation. (Jean Buridan, *Buridan's Ass*)

Recently, our organization conducted a board retreat to plan for the future of Haiti Alive. It was led by a strategic planning professional. This retreat was to begin planning for the future of this nonprofit beyond my wife and me, cofounders of Haiti Alive. We want the ministry to last beyond our lives, and we need to plan for what that looks like. This is one example of how I'm not anti-planning. The planning that is done for Haiti Alive ensures that good work will continue to be done.

## 3. Start small, tell the story, and expect big things.

What do you care about, deeply care about? Is there something you can do to support that passion that helps others? It doesn't have to lead to setting up a nonprofit organization. It can be advocating, making calls, sending emails, giving funds, talking about the ministry with your friends, or volunteering your time.

I believe this to the core, that God put me in the right place, and that I simply tried to respond to the nudge and be faithful. I'm an ordinary person that decided it *was* my problem and that I needed to do something to help. Whether you are an ordinary or extraordinary person, you can do something. We started giving out a handful of school scholarships, we sent money for medications, we tried to feed kids and the elderly, and we supported small projects. Now we have a two-level school that will serve kids in grades 1 through 9, two clinics (one that we're trying to make self-sustaining and the other a free clinic), an elderly feeding program, a program that gives out school supplies to two thousand kids each fall, a Christmas program (providing a meal, a small toy, and a fun day) that attracts over one thousand kids each year, and we are now beginning to build homes in a women's village (with space for sixty-four houses). This ministry has grown far beyond what I could have ever imagined.

■ ■ ■

My encouragement to you is to start small and to tell the story. I had a furniture salesman tell me that when you are at the point that you are completely sick of your store's jingle, only 50 percent of the people have heard it.

Tell the story. Tell the story. Tell the story. Even when you think it's to the point of being annoying—tell the story. It amazes me how many people deeply connected to our ministry for years, will say, "I didn't know you did that" regarding a major facet of our work. It's the "jingle principle." Keep playing the jingle!

Above all, don't manipulate the story; the story should sell itself. There is no need to be disingenuous; your story will appeal to the right people.

Always have the next big project in mind. When I was doing foundation work for the church, I'd ask pastors and committees, "What would you do with a $100,000 gift?" Churches need to understand that they are likely to be the beneficiaries of estate or will giving that they know nothing about. People also have more confidence to leave future gifts when a church has plans and dreams for the future.

Our foundation held onto a $25,000 gift from a donor until a certain church came up with a plan to use the funds. Despite numerous reminders, after one year the church couldn't come up with a plan, so the funds were channeled to another ministry.

Never stop singing your jingle. You must be active on social media; it's simply where some people receive their information. In addition to social media, we send a digital newsletter about four times a year. I speak or preach at as many places or churches that will have me. To make your story and mission known, send news releases to newspaper and media outlets. Although many won't publish, do it anyway. Make sure your board is telling others how wonderful and impactful your organization is to the world.

---

All people are people but not all people are the same.
*(Tout moun se moun, tout moun pa menm.)*

---

It's important to realize that not all people can or will support your organization. One book that was helpful for me to read was *The Seven Faces of Philanthropy: A New Approach to Cultivating Major Donors* by Russ Alan Prince and Karen Maru File, who point out that donors are often motivated by certain types and means of giving. There are people who largely give to religious organizations. There are those who support their alma mater and primarily give to universities or schools. There are also "communitarians" who are often local business owners. They give back to the organizations that support them in their community.

The reality is that some may not give to your charity. It's OK. They're not your people and they are doing good works elsewhere.

One question that I get somewhat regularly is, "Why don't you work here [meaning locally or within the United States]?—we have hungry people here." My response to this question is typically, "It sounds as if you might be called to help those people. Go for it." We must be careful of using that kind of question to avoid doing something to help—here or there or anywhere.

I have a friend who works in Liberia. He said that when he gets that kind of question his response is, "If you'd go to Liberia, you'd understand." Love that response.

A man once told me that he would never give to us because during a period of his life he had to eat out of dumpsters. He didn't like my response, which was, "At least you had dumpsters to eat out of. They don't exist in Haiti."

Lest you think I'm an insensitive jerk, please know that all hunger and being relegated to eating from a dumpster is unconscionable. I admit I probably could have handled this more tactfully, but it demonstrates how many don't understand what poverty looks like in developing countries such as Haiti. There is no backup system. They don't have food stamps or soup kitchens or regular food giveaways. There aren't even dumpsters, and many don't eat every day and are frequently on the edge of starvation.

---

## The more people understand what you do and trust you, the more they will give.

---

What I've found over the years is that generous people are generous to a variety of charities. The more people understand what you do and trust you, the more they will give. One encouragement for your nonprofit is not to fall in love with events. Some go from golf tournament to fishing derby to banquet to poker run to 5K race to . . . whatever is the flavor of the month. Events are great for getting your name out to the public and building a tradition, but they take a tremendous amount of time and staff resources. Is it worth two months of planning for $2,000? For heaven's sake, go ask two of your supporters to each give you a grand. Like planning, events can become an excuse for the hard work on getting out to meet your donors and connecting them to your ministry.

Then, expect big things. If you're a religious person, I would strongly encourage you to pray for your needs. I pray continually for God to find a way. It has happened so often that I've actually come to expect that when we have a need, someone will respond.

I had been thinking about the Women's Village for years. Haiti is a male dominated society, but the women typically bear all responsibility. They work incredibly hard, raising and trying to feed their families, but often they have little support. Many women live in deplorable conditions. There is a mudflat area on LaGonave near the ocean, called The Saline, and families are allowed to obtain land there for free, because it's miserable. When it rains or hurricanes pass over the island, The Saline becomes a muck fest. We have provided some individual homes, when we had funds, but building an entire village was just a dream. That dream took almost ten years to become a reality. But it was the next big thing. After the clinic and school and feeding program and . . . the outreach continues.

## 4. Focus on extreme accountability.

Our finances are an open book. I've actually sent our spreadsheet to donors with individual names removed. Our Board reviews our financial statements, and we use a CPA to file our annual 990 report, because we want that additional level of accountability.

When a donor designates funds for a particular use, you have an obligation to use funds as the donor directs you. If they give money for the feeding program, you can't use it for the school, even if you're low on funds in that account.

Remember that donors have very different personalities. When I was with a certain foundation, a woman called me to berate me for not printing a front-page notice in our newsletter about her $1,000 gift. This call came a day after receiving a $100,000 gift from a woman that refused any kind of recognition. Just be honest with the donor. If someone wants to give a designated donation and you have a great need elsewhere, tell them you have a specific need and ask if you can use the gift in the needed way? If not, thank them and assure them by saying their gift will be used as they have designated.

I've said this to people on LaGonave often, "There are two things that quickly evaporate in Haiti—rain and money. People in the United States are very generous, but if they feel the money is being wasted the money dries up tomorrow."

A few years ago, Dr. William came up with a great plan, to hire an accountant in LaGonave. When sending money, I first email three people in Haiti—William, our accountant, and another Haiti board member. That way three people know the amount of money being sent and the intended use of the funds.

We had a leader that we found was making deals with suppliers. Our leader would say to a supplier, for example, charge $5 more per bag of cement and we'll split the overage. It was one of the most painful moments in my ministry. Someone we had trusted, someone who represented our organization was siphoning off funds. So, we took steps to mitigate the unexpected.

We don't have someone on the ground in Haiti. We have trust in our leaders but we put safeguards in place. We've set up a Haiti Alive Board in Haiti in addition to our Haiti Alive Board here in the United States. We've taken steps to make sure funds don't evaporate.

I trust Dr. William implicitly. He's been to the U.S. several times, so we talk details in person and visit almost daily online. We have had difficult and brutally honest conversations. I trust him because he has given his own funds to support our ministry. He and his wife bought a small piece of land near our school, because we didn't have funds at the time. He was the one who came up with the accountability plan, partially to protect himself from accusation and to protect the use of our funds. Now we've begun to have conversations along the lines of how we would replace William if he were no longer able to assist our organization.

While expensive, it is nice to bring William to the States on occasion. For churches and donors to see him and listen to him gives people the satisfaction of knowing he is real, the ministry is real. He can answer questions more accurately about Haiti and what is happening in the daily lives of the people we serve.

As your ministry or nonprofit grows consider:

Who are your promoters, the story tellers for your good work?
Who may be hurting or hindering your ministry?
How can you reach more people with the good you are doing?
What's your why? Why do you exist?

We've had ups and downs in our ministry. Some have been amazing, some scary, some holy, some poignant, some heartbreaking, but all are part of the story of Haiti Alive.

Chapter Seven

# MISSION TEAMS & GROWTH

The way you come is the way people will receive.

*(Jan ou vini se jan an yo resevwa ou.)*

It's always interesting to see Haiti through the eyes of first timers. From the time we arrive at the chaotic airport, to the crazy busy roads through Port-au-Prince, to the "tap-taps" (basically taxis but highly decorated trucks and backs of pickups), to overloaded vehicles full of people and items going to market, to getting on a boat to cross the bay to LaGonave, to seeing a beautiful Caribbean island as a backdrop to abject poverty—newcomers from the United States who arrive to serve in Haiti are wide-eyed.

We try to hold a processing time as a group for the teams every evening, asking questions like, What did you see or learn? Where did you see God today? What questions do you have? We sometimes bring a "book of questions" as an icebreaker for the teams to get to know one another. Teams may come as strangers but always leave as friends.

We are fixers in the United States. We tend to approach things with the idea that we can make changes that will result in doing things better or making things more efficient. But as my father often says, our role is not to criticize or compare but rather to appreciate and understand.

> ## Our role is not to criticize or compare but rather to appreciate and understand.

My constant reminder to short-term mission teams is, we don't live here. Our role is to learn, not to judge. I also stress that the project we'll work on is the *least* important thing of the trip. It's more important to get to know these kind, funny, generous, interesting, and faithful Haitian people. I encourage everyone to try and learn some of the Creole language—Haitians will appreciate and find humor in your efforts–but remember to communicate in ways other than words. A smile goes a long way, indicating acceptance, encouragement, and love.

Being on a team creates a bond. It also solidifies supporters of your ministry; team members return home and report that the ministry is vital and great things are happening. Those testimonies build legitimacy and connection to our work.

In my own experience and in those of others, the impact of a trip really hits a couple of weeks after returning home. Your friends and family care and are interested, but they really can't fully understand. There are a lot of emotions that are hard to manage, and I always let teams know that I'm only a call or email away. Regrouping as a team stateside after a mission trip can be beneficial.

If at all possible, travel with family. My wife wasn't sure she could handle the travel to Haiti and accommodations, but she finally said, "I need to get to know these people you keep talking about." She's been to Haiti at least five times now, and I've also been able to share the experience with both of our sons.

Unfortunately, we've not been able to bring teams to Haiti since 2020. The pandemic and the rampant increase in gang control of the country has made team travel difficult and dangerous. We can fly into Port-au-Prince and then take a small plane to LaGonave, but we can't stay overnight or travel the roads around Port-au-Prince. Recently, Mission Aviation Fellowship, who would fly these small planes to LaGonave, has left Haiti for now.

The summary below details what has happened in the course of the development of our ministry. Nonprofits go through stages, and hopefully these overviews will help demonstrate how our ministry has changed and grown.

## Education

We began giving scholarships to students to attend school. People in Haiti suggested who should receive these scholarships. We focused largely on kids to attend elementary school. The school system in Haiti is Pre-School/Kindergarten, Elementary from grades 1–9, and Secondary includes grades 10–13. Technical Education and University Education is available, largely in Port-au-Prince.

Most schools are private and/or religious-sponsored schools. There are public schools, but they tend to be woefully funded and have teachers who show up randomly. I always found it funny that they cancel school when it rains. I understand during a hurricane, but apparently, Haitians don't like getting wet walking to school.

In the vast majority of schools, the students wear uniforms, so you can identify which school they go to by the color of their shirt, pants, or skirt, along with the hair adornments that girls love to wear. Many schools serve a meal, which encourages kids to show up each day. The school year schedule is similar to the U.S. schools, from September to June, but with many breaks during the year. A school day typically runs from 7 a.m. to 1 p.m., sending everyone home before the afternoon sun bakes them.

Over the years we have paid tuition for students to attend Technical School or University. We've learned that we need to be selective with such scholarships. Unless our organization is going to hire them after a scholarship recipient graduates, we typically can't feel confident supporting the student. Unfortunately, few students who graduate can otherwise find employment.

Haiti Alive had been supporting an increasing number of students with school scholarships. I had this wonderfully naïve idea; we should build a school. My thought was, we could just chip away at a school building when we had funding, and open the school whenever it was completed. It's so much better to be naïve and lucky, than to be smart.

As were making plans to build the school, Dr. William called me and said, "I think we should name the school after Rob Marchand." Rob was my best friend who died of cancer. It blew me away because William never met Rob, but obviously he knew how important he was to me. The official name, with guidance from the Ministry of Education, became the Rob Marchand Institute (see map in appendix A).

Rob ran a recreation center and was deeply involved in the life of kids. He was a great connector and cared deeply about making the world a better place for the kids that came into the center. Interestingly, Rob thought I should work locally instead of in Haiti, as he just saw so much pain and need in the States. I wish I could have hauled him along on a trip to Haiti.

After a conversation with the family, we decided that Rob's legacy could live on through the school. We announced the name of the school, and in February 2017, we organized a team to help dig the foundation. More accurately, we turned over a few shovels of dirt alongside the hard-working Haitians. We brought some pictures and notes from the family to put into the first blocks to be laid in the school.

About one year after the groundbreaking, we had the funds to complete the first level of the school. Five rooms, and we started with grades 1–3 and a principal's office. The school became a perfect way for people to show their appreciation of Rob. We received few large gifts, but we received enough small gifts to reach our goal.

Rob's son, Jay, and I were invited to a church to talk about the school and our ministry in Haiti. This church was in a sermon series on the Beatitudes and the theme that Sunday was "Blessed are those that mourn, for they shall be comforted." Mourning is a strange animal. We want the world to stop and take notice, but the world keeps turning. We want others to feel our pain, but they move on with their busy lives. It's hard to know how to care for the surviving family, what to say, or how to express our sorrow adequately.

This school has kept the memory of Rob alive and has helped me to mourn. I think it has helped the family too. In September 2018, Rob's wife, two kids, a high school friend, my wife and I went to dedicate the Rob Marchand Institute. I get tears in my eyes thinking about celebrating the opening of the school surrounded by the kids and staff.

## HAITI REFLECTION
### Kevin—Team Member, Friend of Rob

If a family had a child in school, this was and continues to be the greatest hope for their future. I loved seeing the place in the name of my buddy; I felt excited for the kids and their new school. I know so many of them have no way out, unless there is a dream planted somewhere.

We planned to add one grade a year, so the first level quickly filled up. We needed to start building the second level with five more rooms. Again, people responded.

The roof of the first level became the floor of the second level. In 2019, the second level appeared, and we completed the roof in August 2019. The school was basically completed.

Since that time, we've built a wall around the school, added a computer lab, constructed a system to collect rainwater off the roof to flow into a cistern, added a kitchen with storage area, and purchased a bus. Buying a bus in Florida and transporting it to Haiti was an adventure of epic proportions, but we have students that live a long way from the school, and now they have transportation.

We held some interesting fundraisers for the sake of the school (see appendix C). Again, we received many small gifts to build the school. Our scholarship program gives us funds to buy uniforms, provide meals for students, and the materials necessary to educate students. We have eighteen people (teachers, principal's office, nurse, cooks, security, bus driver) that receive monthly income for their work in the ministry plus twelve people we contract to teach specific courses. This allows our Haitian staff to care for their own families.

We paid local workers to build the school so they could earn money and have pride in their accomplishment. Concrete on LaGonave is mixed on the ground with shovels and carried bucket by bucket. Blocks are made by hand. The roof is high from the ground. When I think about how much work it took to make this beautiful school, I stand in amazement.

As a former educator, giving students an opportunity to learn is a treasure for me. A few years ago, we started a "Back to School Program" by giving pens, pencils, and notebooks to up to two thousand children each fall. Many schools and families aren't able to provide basic supplies, so we've tried to fill that gap. I love that education is one of our priorities. (See pictures in appendix D.)

## HAITI REFLECTION
### Sophie—Team Member

We had just finished our work for the day, painting the exterior of the school. We had given out gifts of schoolbooks, but they *loved* it when we brought out the bottles of bubbles. With pure joy they laughed and chased the bubbles, kids being kids. I had this wave of emotion as we left in the back of the pickup that day. They were so happy with the little that they received.

## Healthcare

In 2016, Dr. William completed his five-year program at UTESA Medical School, Santiago, Dominican Republic. This was an amazing accomplishment! William was chosen by his classmates to assign the medical rotations. A beautiful Haitian woman, Nathalie, was curiously assigned to all his rotations. Dr. William and Dr. Nathalie were married in 2018.

We were honored to be invited to William's graduation. The saying "it takes a village" so aptly applies here. To begin with, a village of people provided financial support for William's school and living expenses. But we discovered other villages of support.

William and three friends moved into an apartment in Santiago, and it was scary for them. They didn't know the language or how to navigate this new city and country. A wonderful *abuela* (grandmother) took them under her wing. She showed them where to go, how to buy food and other essentials, how to get transportation, helped them with the language, and she even cleaned their apartment from time to time. She was part of the village.

The Sunday morning after graduation we went to a Haitian church in Santiago. While we didn't understand much of the language, the energy was captivating. Their songs, prayers, and sermons were given with such enthusiasm and spirit. It is not uncommon for church services to last three or more hours. At the end of the worship, all the students that had graduated the night before and their families were invited up to the front of the church to be recognized. It was very obvious that this church community had cared for William and many other students. Another village of support.

Sunday evening was the graduation celebration. Many people in attendance stood and talked about William, including his uncle, who took William in when he was orphaned after William's mom died; friends from Haiti who saw him grow and mature and were proud that he would return home to help their native country; fellow students who talked about their friendships and going through trials and triumphs together; and several Dominican families who had adopted these Haitian students into their lives, so much so that William was asked to be the godfather of one of the babies who was at the party.

During medical school, William organized mobile clinics in the Dominican Republic to areas called *bateys*, which are slums where Haitian workers live. The mobile clinics would bring clothes, food, and basic medical supplies. William also worked alongside our medical teams that came to Haiti.

We realized we needed a place for a clinic on the island. There are approximately 80,000 people that live on LaGonave and most of them live in the city of Anse-a-Galets. This is the largest city, by far, and it's where the hospital is located along with most of the businesses and resources on the island. Our plan was to bring medical care to the rural areas.

We took a team to Nan Café in 2012, which is a village up the mountain. It's a beautiful area, with more variety in crops, more vegetation, better water supply, a bit cooler, but it's an arduous trip to get there. Some of the worst roads you've been on are some of the best roads on LaGonave. It's a two-and-a-half- to three-hour trip up the hill to Nan Café.

Our project in Nan Café was to put a new roof on a church. We also decided to buy land for a clinic near the church (that we later found out we grossly overpaid for!) and began making plans. It eventually became clear that we couldn't afford to put a clinic in that location. We've tried to sell the land but have, in essence, given it to the church and asked them to make it available for people to plant crops.

## Placing the Clinics

About 10 miles west of Anse-a-Galets is the village of Zetwa. It's at an intersection of two or three roads to the remote parts of the island. We purchased a house that we converted into a clinic. A team from South Dakota came to make improvements to the clinic, including a bathroom and additional space.

That ten miles to the clinic takes at least 45 minutes to transport clinic staff, and the numbers of patients coming to our clinic began to decline. It is expensive to transport staff, and many of these people from the village were going to Anse-a-Galets for their medical care. William suggested to close this clinic and build a clinic onto the end of the school. Our school is on the edge of the main town, and we could continue to provide free care to people in a more centralized area.

William's idea led to a great decision. We began receiving many patients and are already considering how we can increase our clinic space. With the help of a church and donors, William built another clinic in Anse-a-Galets. The idea was this would be a for-pay clinic, for those who can afford medical care, and the clinic by the school would be a free clinic, but they'd work together.

Recent difficulties in the country have required financial assistance to pay medical staff salaries in the for-pay clinic, but appreciate William is working to make that clinic financially self-sufficient. Clinics are expensive ventures, especially the need to resupply the pharmacy and other equipment. Currently, six medical staff are paid between the two clinics.

We have had several medical teams come from the United States to support the medical ministry and their work always amazes me. I look at a patient and think, if our team wouldn't have been there, that person would have died. We also found that we need to purchase medicines in Haiti. For example, we have better medications for high blood pressure, and they work well. But they aren't available in Haiti. If we start someone on a med and then a month or two later, they can't get the same prescription, it's not good for the patient.

Our Haiti medical staff has also tried to respond to local issues. Our team brought medical and relief supplies to the south part of Haiti after a large earthquake in 2021. There was also a large scabies outbreak and our Haiti Alive medical team brought relief. There have been sporadic epidemics of cholera and we've responded. When we have funds, we send mobile clinics to the rural villages where they have very little access to medical care.

## HAITI REFLECTION
### Jan—Team Member, Pharmacist

We gave away lots of free medicine, but they seemed to like the peanut butter on bread better. They were so hungry, but happy to receive one meal a day. We take medicine and food for granted.

## Women in Haiti

Women are the lifeblood, literally, of families. They work so hard and carry much of the burden. As I have written, it's a male-dominated society, so many women live a hard life. Hygiene, childbearing, and child-caring are critical issues for women.

We've done small things for women's groups over the years. Our Haiti Board identifies women and families who have "no possibilities" so we help them with food giveaways. We've considered some training programs, like our purchasing of sewing machines so women can learn a trade.

We're beginning a microloan program. With a generous donation, we will have a team provide training to women, and funds for the women to begin a small business. Our goal is for the program to be self-sustaining with the payback of loans. But more importantly, create an avenue for women to provide for themselves and their families.

Due to a large gift from an anonymous donor, we were able to buy a large tract of land. We were also put in contact with an organization who had an engineer with a great track record for building homes as well as a great process for home construction. The engineer trains a group of foremen. These foremen are provided the house plan, the materials, and a sum of money for labor. These bosses can hire as many or as few workers as they decide, as the money for labor is set. The materials are provided and if, for example, they find they are short a couple bags of cement, the boss is responsible.

It puts the onus on the bosses and workers, so construction materials don't disappear. The engineer is there to supervise, help, and educate the bosses. If the boss and workers build a home on budget and construction is done well, they get another home to build. We began building in the fall of 2022 and the land has room for 64 houses, and we're well on the way toward that number. We've also been able to give around 100 workers an income to feed their own families.

The homes will be given to the women; we don't want to become landlords and the women will have an asset for their future. They will need to understand and sign an agreement that the home can never be owned by a man, and they can lose the home if they can't live peacefully with others in the Women's Village community.

There is a committee in Haiti that review applications for the homes. They will make sure the women have actual need, that the woman can live up to the agreements of the village, and the committee is also relegated with the difficult decision of choosing the women. We've received over three hundred applications for homes and that number is climbing.

One amazing feature is that the homes will have indoor, flush toilets. Four homes will share a septic tank system. Most of the people living in these homes will have never used a flush toilet before in their life. We have a team of women who will teach the families how to use a toilet.

We've had a few bumps, but it's been an amazing project. The mayor of Anse-a-Galets has been so impressed that he has identified a piece of land they will give us when we have completed the first Women's Village. They want us to build a market area, as the village is located some distance outside of the main town. These are future dreams!

The cost of each home is currently $11,500, but the cost of materials continues to climb. It's a significant amount of money but think of the impact that home ownership has on a woman and her family. The generous gifts of the anonymous donors and other home sponsors have made this dream an incredible reality.

My nightmare began in 2012. I was having an emergency C-section to deliver my twins and found out my husband had died suddenly. We moved from the south of LaGonave to Anse-a-Galets to find work. I clean houses or wash clothes in exchange for money or food for me and my family [of twelve children]. But I can't always find work. Life is hard and someday my situation will change for the better. I can't thank you enough for this house—a roof over our head that will lighten my burden and the pain for my family. God bless you.

—Merilia

My mother passed away when I was fourteen, so I had to move in with my father. He was a fisherman, so at least we had food on the table every day. At eighteen, I got pregnant, but my boyfriend denied it was his and abandoned me. This has been a bad cycle for me. I now have five children from five fathers and each time the fathers left me. I have no money to pay for a place to live. Haiti Alive is changing lives and you are blessing my family and other families more than you can know. Thank you so much and God bless all of you.

—Carline

## Children in Haiti

The earthquake occurred in January of 2010, and as Christmas was nearing later that year, William suggested a Christmas Party, as the people needed joy. The first couple of years, we focused on orphans as the recipients of that Christmas joy, children near and dear to William. We've held Haiti Children Christmas each year since, giving out small toys, a meal, treating them to a fun program of music and singing, and letting them know that Christ and others care for them. This past year we had over 1,200 kids, and the entire program was shown online by a local news outlet.

We've tried to do a weekly feeding program for children. Recently, this has not happened as much as we'd like. Food has gotten ridiculously expensive on LaGonave and we're doing what we can to make sure our school kids get fed every day.

## Elderly in Haiti

As I had mentioned, growing old in Haiti poses great difficulty, and the elderly have become a focus for our teams. One night, after we'd given away food and clothes to the elderly, a woman came to our gate and wanted to see me. She handed me a small plastic bag and wanted me to thank the team for the items she was given that day. When she left, I opened the bag to find seeds. There is a tree similar to a honey locust, with seeds in long pods. She had removed the seeds from the pods to offer me a gift. It was what she had. It was a gift that I will forever treasure, a gift given out of appreciation and love.

We had started receiving food packets from organizations like Kids Against Hunger and Mercy Meals. They are rice-based packs, with protein, vitamins, and minerals created by food scientists. When prepared, one cup from the packet provides all the daily nutrition. At first our elderly friends didn't like them—until they started feeling better. Typically, we have just provided rice and beans, the common daily food of Haitians, but the food packets include the protein and nutrients needed for hungry and starving people.

We also have used these packets for our school lunch and feeding programs. As of this writing, we haven't been able to get packets into the country because of the instability in Port-au-Prince. We have a sea container of packets that are ready to be sent if we can get the ports open and some stability and safety for shipping and unloading. Not being able to receive packets is impacting the people of LaGonave greatly, especially the elderly.

The way you come is the way you will be received. Who are these people and what do their daily lives look like? (See images of Haiti in appendix D.)

Chapter Eight

# DAILY LIFE IN HAITI

Live today, but think about tomorrow.

*(Viv jodia, men reflechi sou demen.)*

Did you eat breakfast or lunch today? What if I said your next meal would be breakfast or lunch tomorrow—24 hours later? That's daily life for many in Haiti. Frankly, I don't know how some stay alive. Depending on sources, 60 to 80 percent of the people in Haiti don't have regular employment or income. Many rely on agriculture—growing a crop and then selling it to others, until there's a drought or a hurricane that washes the crop away or it's unsafe to travel to a marketplace.

One day we were walking to the worksite and my interpreter (Mr. B) stopped a small girl on the path. He took a granola bar out of his pocket and offered it to the girl. She shook her head and started to walk on. The interpreter asked her to stop and basically forced her to take the granola bar.

"Why her?" I asked, thinking there were many other kids we passed on the trail.

"Because she's a *restavek* [a child slave]," he said.

"How do you know?"

"Because I was one too," Mr. B replied.

**The Story of Mr. B**

According to *Restavek Freedom*, an organization with the mission of ending child slavery in Haiti, there are an estimated 300,000 children, 60 percent of which are girls, who are *restaveks*. The word means "to stay with" but it is much worse. A typical scenario: parents from a rural area send their child to a family in an urban area. The parents are promised their child will be cared for and receive an education. There is a higher chance that the child will be physically, emotionally, and sexually abused.

Mr. B told me what it was like to be a child slave. He was forced to work for relatives who made him care for the gardens, clean, and prepare food for the family. He was fed only from the scraps of their meals. One day they told him to climb a coconut tree. Mr. B complained he was too young, and the tree was too high. To no avail he was forced to climb the tree—and he fell. He broke his wrist and leg and never saw a doctor. He walks with a limp to this day.

Mr. B escaped from the family and snuck onto a boat to come to the United States. The boat was intercepted and he spent time in Guantanamo. He failed the exit interview, so he changed his name and interviewed again. He lived in the United States for about fifteen years but made some poor choices and was deported back to Haiti. When he was returned to a Haiti prison, he said it was the closest he had ever come to dying, with violence rampant along with overcrowding and under feeding.

What is your typical day like? For most of us, it doesn't compare to the day of a restavek.

## Sharing With Others

On our trips to LaGonave, I'm amazed at how the kids share with each other. If we give out granola bars or candy, they will always share with a friend first before eating it themselves. If I was starving and only ate one meal a day, would I share food given to me? I doubt it.

In one of our clinics, a nursing mother was obviously malnourished. The doctor gave her a few Power Bars and a couple bottles of water. The woman put the bars in her pocket, but the doctor said to eat the bar now and I'll give you another. This starving woman was saving food for her children.

## A Passionate People

It is a competitive society, Haiti, and I suppose that stems from an extreme lack of resources. Haitians are passionate and vocal people. On a boat ride across the bay, two men were yelling at each other and being very demonstrative. A worried team member asked me if everything was OK. I asked the two men, "Politics or soccer?" They laughed and responded, "Soccer." Those two subjects always lead to heated discussions.

In Haiti people love to tease each other and laugh. One of the downfalls of not knowing the language well is we miss some of those interactions. There have been few days that I've spent on LaGonave that haven't been filled with laughter.

The people of Haiti take pride in their appearance. Unless they are desperately poor, their clothing is always clean and bright. If someone falls during soccer, other kids will come to help them swat the dust off their clothes. I have this enduring image from one of my first trips. It was raining lightly, the ground was muddy, and between two buildings this woman was walking to church in a beautiful, bright, white dress. How could she look so clean in this place? Our visiting mission teams are often the mutts in church; most Haitians wear suitcoats and dresses to worship.

## Day to Day Life

Market places are busy, interesting places. Because most people don't have refrigeration, food is purchased daily from the market. They are the "Wal-Marts" of Haiti. You can find everything from medications to oil to clothing to fruits and vegetables to meat to daily staples like rice and beans. Large towns have markets every day, and they are held once or twice a week in more rural areas. The "meat counter" is a place I try to avoid. Chickens or goats are slaughtered on site and the price goes down the longer they sit in the hot sun. The flies and smell are a bit overwhelming.

Another item that is found in the market is charcoal. It is fascinating to watch a Haitian create a charcoal burn. Sticks are meticulously placed in a pile that looks like an oversized loaf of French bread. Then the pile is covered with soil and leaves and ignited. Smoke plumes can often be seen across the hillsides. After a week or so, the pile is taken apart by shovels to bag up what remains, the charcoal. Bags that are 4 to 5 feet long are filled with the black pieces and head to market to be sold. It's easy to say they need to stop cutting down trees for this practice, but what if that's one's only source of income? I see more bottle gas being used, but charcoal is the traditional method, and many can't afford a gas stove.

In 2013, I put together a picture and reflection booklet called *I Saw God Today.* This was one of my reflections regarding the role the donkey plays in life in Haiti:

> I saw God today in the donkey. I'm not sure there is an animal that works as hard as the donkey. In a place with little water or food, the donkey gets loaded down with huge bags of charcoal, piles of bananas, wood, or sometimes the owner. The person guiding the donkey frequently has a whip to coax the beast to continue in the right direction. When we went to the market, there was a "donkey parking lot" where they wait for more work later in the day. A missionary said to me once, the work that you do needs to always be about God and not about you as a person. So the donkey is a great role model, who keeps their heads down and plods along day after day. The donkey occasionally needs some direction but does the heavy lifting without needing recognition. I saw God in the donkey today who teaches me where to keep my focus.

Most Haitians eat rice and beans every day. The most common proteins are fish, chicken, and goat. There are locally grown fruits, including banana, plantain, watermelon, and the mangoes are simply amazing. Coffee is grown in parts of LaGonave, and most Haitians drink their coffee with many spoonsful of sugar. New Years is celebrated with a traditional pumpkin soup.

Clean water is an issue on the island. There are places that sell water that has gone through reverse osmosis, but many cannot afford it. A Wesleyan Church water initiative brings spring water from the hills to pumps or well areas in Anse-a-Galets, where people fill up containers for their daily use. But the water isn't purified or treated, so it isn't safe for our teams. Unfortunately, water isn't always safe for Haitians either, which is why they have bouts of cholera and other intestinal problems.

## Transportation across the Island

Transportation across LaGonave is difficult. Most roads are rugged and rocky. The main way to get around on this island is by motorcycle. I've seen four kids and a driver on a motorcycle delivering them to a school. It's expensive to bring vehicles to Haiti and then finally to LaGonave, and most don't do well with the terrain. We run our bus down the main road of Anse-a-Galets, a small section that is paved in concrete, to bring kids from up to two miles from the school. We have a hard time keeping the bus going; the roads are hard on tires and when parts fail, they have to be ordered from Port-au-Prince or sometimes the States.

We've had some interesting experiences for teams. We were taking the "Jesus boat" back to the mainland in ten- to twelve-foot swells in the bay. Every time I saw a new wave, I thought, man there are going to be some families unhappy with me if this boat swamps. One of our team members, Tammy, was wearing an adorable, printed dress with matching headband. After the trip she, and all the rest of us, didn't look so adorable.

There was a team that couldn't get to the airport due to protests along the road to Port-au-Prince. They had to arrange for a special boat and an armored vehicle to get them to the airport. On one trip we got to the airport and found out that a gun battle

happened just fifteen minutes after we were inside. Fifteen minutes later and we might not have made it to the airport.

We were stopped on the main road to Port-au-Prince by men
who were shirtless, wore grass skirts, and wore masks. It was
intimidating as they stopped and approached our van. They were
asking for money from our driver for the Haiti Carnival celebration that leads up to Mardi Gras or Lent.

As I mentioned, currently it is not at all safe to travel around
Port-au-Prince. Gang control of the city is threatening and
heart-breaking.

## Religious Belief

Most people here identify as Christian but hold on to traditional
beliefs. In early trips, there were traveling voodoo groups, and
you could hear drumming and chanting until the wee hours of
the night.

## HAITI REFLECTION
### Merle—Team Member

We've seen the presence of black magic or voodoo. People
feel the threat of bad spells being placed on them when
someone is jealous of their position or wants to harm
them.

The church services in Haiti are high energy and long. A typical service will last up to three hours. The first time William went

with me to a church service in the United States, he looked puzzled when the service ended and asked, "Finished already?" I'm always humbled by the faith of the Haitian people. I've wondered if this faith stems from having a tough life on earth, so the promise of a better afterlife engenders their faith.

I was preaching at a church one time with an interpreter. It's always a dance between speaking with an interpreter on how much to say before waiting to have the phrase interpreted for the people. I said a short sentence and the interpreter went on for probably two minutes. I said, "Wow. I must have been great." The translator laughed. "I forgot I was speaking for you; I was speaking for God." Hard to argue with that.

## Soccer

If you want to make friends on LaGonave, pack along a soccer ball. They are literally "gold" and the most coveted thing we bring. Soccer is huge in Haiti, while baseball is the game in the Dominican Republic. I've seen just about anything used to make soccer balls—clothes, twine, plastic, anything that can be formed into something basically round. With the rocky ground, our soccer balls don't usually last long and the kids often play barefoot.

There are soccer fields across LaGonave and intense competition. The people are passionate about local, regional, national, and international teams. My son was at a soccer field when the bleachers collapsed. He remembers "surfing" down on pieces of wood and then helping to pull people out of the entanglement. Amazingly no one was seriously injured.

## Bringing Hope

What I've come to learn is that our teams and the funding of projects bring hope. It's a precious commodity in this country. Haitians have no choice but to live for today, but we help them to have hope for tomorrow.

I have yet to meet someone who didn't come away from a trip without a fresh perspective and appreciation for the people that live in Haiti. One of my favorite team stories was included in my last book, *Mighty Winds & Gentle Whispers: The Purpose & Power of the Holy Spirit:*

> One afternoon we traveled up the mountain to a small village. Local doctors were holding a mobile clinic, and we went up to observe and to bring medical supplies and food. We loaded up supplies and seven of us in the back of a pickup. Now, the worst roads you've been on are some of the best on La Gonâve. It is a rocky, volcanic island, and the roads are almost indescribable. It took more than two hours to go about fifteen miles to this village.
>
> About an hour into our journey, it began raining [and] we were soaked to the core. After we arrived at the clinic, we gave out food and medical supplies and observed some of the difficult medical cases. [Once we were done and the rain had let up, we headed back] down the mountain. Not ten minutes into our trip, it began to rain [heavily again].
>
> [Throughout this cold and wet journey] I was sitting on the back corner of the pickup along with my pastor friend. He and I could see the water cascading down the road behind

us. It looked like a waterfall, water pouring over the rocks and chasing us down the hill. [We] turned to look at each other and just laughed. We'd look at other team members, drowned rats in the back of a pickup, and just laugh. A time when people could have been angry or disappointed or frustrated, and all we could do was laugh.

My pastor friend recalled this as his memorable event. He said he will use this memory when the sky is falling on him, when things are dark and bleak, when he is soaked from the problems of others—he can choose to laugh. Through it all, things will be better. The rain will stop. We can laugh.

Once we were preparing for a trip to Haiti when our grandkids came over; they were seven and four at the time. They handed us this small, red, drawstring bag. I opened it and saw some money. They wanted to help pay for our trip. We asked if we could give the money to some kids or buy something for the people there. No, they wanted us to have the money, to help us with the cost of our trip. We were now $1.42 closer to paying for our trip. I think that's the right amount; it's hard to count change with tears in your eyes and a smile on your face.

We often come back from Haiti with tears in our eyes and smiles on our faces. Smiles for the wonderful people we've met and tears for what they have to endure daily.

How did Haiti get to such a difficult place?

Chapter Nine

# HOW DID THEY GET HERE?

Haiti is sliding land [quicksand].

*(Ayiti se te glise).*

People who follow news about Haiti or have been there tend to wonder the same thing: how did Haiti get to this place? Why have they gotten to the place of instability in their government and such need for people throughout the country?

A legitimate question of donors is, have things gotten better? What they are really asking is, does my gift make a difference? My response is, for individuals, yes; for the whole of the country, the jury is still out.

One day a farmer's donkey fell into an abandoned well. Terrified, the animal cried for hours as the farmer tried to figure out what to do. Finally, he decided the animal was old and impossible to retrieve. He realized the well needed to be filled to prevent future losses. So he invited all his neighbors to help him.

They all grabbed shovels and began to throw dirt into the well. At first, when the donkey realized he was being buried alive, he cried horribly. Then, to everyone's shock, the donkey quieted down. A few shovel loads later, the farmer looked down the well and was astonished at what he saw. With each shovel of dirt that hit the donkey's back, the donkey would shake it off and take a step up.

As the farmer and his neighbors continued to throw dirt on top of the animal, he would shake it off and take another step up. Soon everyone was amazed as the donkey stepped up over the edge of the well and happily trotted off!

Life is going to throw dirt your way and attempt to bury you. However, no one ever gets out of life's wells by giving up! Shake the dirt off and take a step up! (https://wisdomshare .com/stories/farmers-donkey/)

The goal for our ministry is that, alongside our neighbors, we try to help shovel by shovel. The resilient people of Haiti shake each tragedy off, and our help allows them to take the next step up. There are people in Haiti that we know and care about and our help makes a difference for them. There are many other non-profits throughout Haiti and the rest of the world that are trying to do the same thing—make a difference person by person.

## A Brief History of Haiti

Haiti and the Dominican Republic share an island called His-paniola. Haiti is on the west end of the island and was settled by the French. The Dominican Republic was settled by the Spanish. These countries, who occupy the land on the same island, have shared experiences but also different histories. There continues to be significant conflict between the two countries to this day.

A book that provides a good perspective on the history of the country is *Haiti: The Tumultuous History—From Pearl of the Caribbean to Broken Nation,* by Philippe Girard. At one time, Haiti was a wealthy country that produced sugar cane, rum, and exported tons of sugar.

Christopher Columbus actually landed near Cap Haitien to establish a settlement. There was an indigenous tribe of Tainos people who weren't pleased and eliminated these newcomers. That prompted a move of the capital to the area around Santo Domingo. But the Columbus landing opened the floodgates for Spain's enslavement of the Taino people. They were forced into labor until the tribe was largely wiped out by European diseases or abuse. To support their need for money and labor, ships began delivering slaves from Africa.

The Spanish handed over control of the area that would become Haiti to the French. On our trip in 2002, we walked up the mountain to the Citadel (*Citadelle* in French), a fortress built by Henri Christophe. Here's a nice summary of its history.

## HAITI REFLECTION
### Michael McEwen Randall

In 1803, after thirteen years of war, Haiti won independence from France. Three years later, Henri Christophe, a former slave and one of the revolution's leaders, declared himself king of northern Haiti. The revolution was utterly brutal, and in subsequent raids against the French colony to the east (today's Dominican Republic) Christophe and his troops committed acts of utter savagery against local people there.

At home, he presided over an unhappy population, angry with his autocratic rule. He became emotionally ill and increasingly distrustful. Tyrannical and probably paranoid, he forced construction of an immense fortress, La Citadelle, from stones and brick and mortar on a mountain top fifteen miles from Cap Haitien. Thousands of forced laborers died during the years-long project.

One day, our group visited Henri Christophe's La Citadelle, which is clearly a monument to his madness. A huge, engineering marvel with rain catchments and aqueducts and a 120-foot-high wall that faces northward across the plains to Cap Haitien. Christophe brought in several architects and engineers from Europe to design and build the massive structure. When the project was finally done, he had them killed. The Citadelle still contains over one hundred cannon and ten thousand cannon balls taken from English, French, and Spanish ships and hauled overland and up the mountain.

Increasingly tormented, isolated from his people and the army, and fearing assassination, Christophe began to make instant decisions about a person's loyalty. Of those he decided were disloyal he gave a choice: be beheaded by a machete or step off a 120-foot-high wall and fall into the boulders and trees below.

His growing derangement and despotism finally drove some of his noblemen and his army into open rebellion. One night in 1820, partially paralyzed by an earlier stroke, Christophe sat atop the Citadelle and watched. Far below him, out on the plains toward Cap Haitien, several plantations were burning. His army was coming for him.

With this clear evidence of his approaching end, he chose to load a silver bullet into his gun. From the traditions and practices of voodoo, he knew what vampires were. Perhaps he had enough remaining remnants of sanity to realize that he had become one of them many years before. Then he shot himself through the heart.

It is estimated that over a half a million slaves would be brought to the island of Hispaniola. Many of them worked in the area that became Port-au-Prince for sugar production and general labor. With the indigenous tribe wiped out, Haiti became largely descendants of slaves.

Slave rebellions led Haiti to become the world's oldest black republic and one of the oldest republics in the Western Hemisphere. Their original constitution called for freedom of religion and not allowing a white person to possess land in the country, to keep the French from reimposing slavery. Suspicion of people from outside the country continues to this day.

Following the Haitian Revolution, France forced Haiti, under the threat of war, to reimburse the people who had enslaved them for the loss of their "property." The sums were huge and hobbled this new government for decades.

The short version of country leadership is, the president/ruler of the country would rule for a period of time, then as they left the country, they would take funds and resources on their way out. Any remaining people from that administration would be killed by the new president/ruler, until *they* left and took money and resources on their way out.

Some of you may remember the Duvalier Era. Francois Duvalier (Papa Doc) established a violent and repressive dictatorship. His private militia, the Tonton Macoutes, promoted widespread intimidation, rape, murders, and the beating of any political opponents. Upon his death, power was transferred to his nineteen-year-old son, Pierre-Claude Duvalier (Baby Doc). While many of the fearsome parts of his father's regime ended, the country continued into economic decline.

For periods of time the military seized control of the country in hopes of establishing a democracy. Jean-Bertrand Aristide, a Roman Catholic priest, won an election handily and was established as president. He was overthrown by a coup and flown to another country in asylum, only later to return to be elected again. Recently, there have been a series of presidential elections that didn't need military intervention in between. But elections are always contentious and divisive.

Jovenel Moise was elected in 2017 to serve until 2021. He refused to step down, due to a discrepancy when he believed his term began. On July 7, 2021, Moise was assassinated in his home and there has not been an election since. The country is being led by the Prime Minister, who is widely unpopular.

Haiti's government makes our own political dissension and controversy look like child's play. This instability has made it virtually impossible to deal with the economic conditions and response to natural disasters. The country had another large earthquake in 2021, and there have been a recurring list of devastating tropical storms and hurricanes. As many say, when will Haiti catch a break?

Gangs have largely taken over control of Port-au-Prince. For a period of time a gang shut down fuel distribution. Gas was over $25 a gallon until they allowed fuel to flow again. One gang tactic to raise funds is to kidnap people and hold them for ransom—not only foreigners, but fellow Haitians. Demonstrations, some that turn ugly, are interspersed with people hiding from the gangs. Virtually all nonprofits have pulled their foreign staff from serving on the ground in Haiti. It's a devastating time.

Throughout history the United States and other countries have forced their will on Haiti. The United States has militarily occupied the country a couple of times. The United Nations provided security forces for a period of time as well but were forced to leave. Large nonprofit organizations have stopped their programming due to instability and security issues.

Outside help is sometimes counterproductive. One of the famous examples is when President Clinton shipped loads of rice to Haiti. It was done for good reasons, but it put local rice farmers out of business. They couldn't compete with the free rice from the States. President Clinton later admitted this was a huge mistake for the development of Haiti. Dr. Paul Farmer lists in his books (*Mountains beyond Mountains* and *Uses of Haiti*) other water and agriculture projects that have hurt more than helped. The Haitian people are suspicious of outside help, even though they've become reliant on those resources.

## No Easy Answers

Haiti is never an easy place to travel to, and travel to LaGonave is even more complicated, as I mentioned earlier. It is more common that the U.S. State Department has high-level travel warnings than not. Since 2020, bringing teams to Haiti has been nearly impossible.

Every time there's an upheaval, there is a diaspora of the best and brightest Haitians out of the country. Those that have connections or resources are the ones that find other countries in which to live. It's understandable, but not good for Haiti. The U.S. Customs and Immigration Services released a new opportunity for citizens of four specific countries—Haiti, Cuba, Nicaragua, and Venezuela. If they can demonstrate they have a financial sponsor, these people can stay in the United States for two years. Another diaspora, and many will never return to their home countries.

One of my observations is that it's hard to collect any tax revenue. If you're selling watermelon in the market, the exchange is between you and your buyer. The government doesn't get any part of that transaction. Hotels, some restaurants, and places that cater to foreign clients do charge taxes, which is completely appropriate, but most exchange throughout the country happens with local vendors along roadsides.

I asked about it once and there is such mistrust of the government, that people said they wouldn't send in tax money, even if they collected it. Many deals are made with officials on taxes owed for land or buildings, so funds end up in officials' pockets and not in the national coffers. Yet people want and expect their government to help them.

I don't have a good answer. I've listened to advocates for the country and even they don't seem to have workable solutions. I do believe the Haitian people need to be responsible for their own future.

This is a familiar story to many of you:

> "I must ask, then, why are you throwing starfish into the ocean?" asked the somewhat startled wise man.
>
> To this, the young man replied, "The sun is up and the tide is going out. If I don't throw them in, they'll die."
>
> Upon hearing this, the wise man commented, "But, young man, do you not realize that there are miles and miles of beach and there are starfish all along every mile? You can't possibly make a difference!"
>
> At this, the young man bent down, picked up yet another starfish, and threw it into the ocean. As it met the water, he said, "It made a difference for that one."
>
> —Loren Eiseley, "The Star Thrower"

The starfish example is one that helps me. There are people that we know and care about in Haiti and many more we hope to meet, and our help makes a difference for them. There are people that are trying to take a step up, until they can walk out of the well by themselves. Until such a time, we and our neighbors will continue to help shovel by shovel, starfish by starfish. Where is your well? Who are your starfish?

Chapter Ten

# IT IS OUR PROBLEM

Little by little the bird builds its nest.

*(Piti piti zwazo fe niche li.)*

The opening page of the Haiti Alive website (www.HaitiAlive
.org) has this proverb and it has guided me over the years—
Little by little the bird builds its nest. My wife, a prolific cross-
stitcher, made a piece with this saying that I had framed to keep the
reminder in front of me. When things get hard or when I become
discouraged, I try to remember that we can't do everything today
but, little by little, we'll get there.

We've come a long way, but the issue that keeps me up at night
now is, how do we maintain what we've built? The school continues to have needs—fix the roof, paint the walls, pave areas that
are dusty, supply and repair desks, provide materials for teachers,
feed the kids, and the list goes on. The clinics have a constant
need for staff, medications, mobile clinic supplies, and to be able
to respond to the needs of the people. The Women's Village has
had some unanticipated costs of streetlights, paving a main road,
security, and we know there will be more in the future.

We're a small nonprofit. Our resources come largely from caring churches and donors. We aren't part of a larger organization

or Conference, so we don't have backup funding. We also know that a "drop and run ministry" isn't who we want to be. What problems are solved if we simply throw money at a problem and then walk away from the people?

Who are we and who should we be as an organization? We have no paid staff, but could we grow if we did? Should we take steps to move from a "mom and pop" nonprofit to a more "mature" organization? What does the future look like for Haiti Alive? What if we lose one or two of our lead donors? It's these questions and more that our board is considering.

I am at the point where I am considering my role. Am I, as the co-founder, contributing to growth or getting in the way of it? When I step away, will the ministry continue, and how will I handle the inevitable changes? I've been connected to organizations where the leader resisted change and made the transition painful. I don't want to be that person.

I've had some unique experiences that changed the trajectory of my life. I was a wide-eyed kid from the Plains, trying to absorb my first global experience in Ghana, then I was a wide-eyed first-timer in Haiti, trying to absorb what this place is all about. Now I just try to keep my eyes wide open to the needs of others.

When I see rhetoric about America Only, I cringe. To assume that we're not connected to the world or that we can hide from the world is naïve. What that rhetoric means is, "It's not my problem."

Look at where the parts are made on your vehicle or other equipment, they come from multiple countries. The stuff we order on Amazon often originates outside the United States. I get a message or contact from Haiti literally every day. The people in Haiti have limited resources, yet I'm in constant communication with people there. We're extravagantly wealthy as a country. How about *and* thinking, that we can care for people here *and* other places?

---

### Don't become comfortable in indifference. It IS my problem. It IS your problem.

---

Matthew West has a song, *Do Something*. It's about a person that sees so much pain and poverty in the world and appeals to God.

I said, "God, why don't You do something?"
[God] said, "I did." Yeah. "I created you."

That's us. God created us to do something. Follow that nudge to do more. It's our problem and now we are going to do something. What about you? What are you interested in or passionate about? Where can you open your eyes and your heart to see?

Hunger bugs me. I've never gone truly hungry in my life. We feed the school kids every day and get meals for the elderly as often as we have funds. Locally, I serve on the board of a food packing organization, Kids Against Hunger, and volunteer time at our state food distribution organization, Feeding South Dakota.

Maybe it's homelessness. Can you advocate with your local and state governments? How about handing out gift cards or bottles of water and, even better, also have a conversation with someone living on our streets and alleys.

How about your church community? I bet they have shut-ins or those that could use a call by phone, someone to send cards of care, or a visit. Every church I know of has needs in their church school ministry or youth ministry. Could you reach out to visitors to your church or start a community group? Can you serve on a committee and encourage them to actually do something other than review the same agenda and minutes for months on end? I'll bet your pastor could find the right place for you.

Is an organized group your thing? Join a civic or service group. Many of them have focus areas like immunizations, eyeglasses, serving youth, or improving the community. There are so many areas. You are needed! Find your calling.

Human trafficking or Sexual Assault Centers care for complex and hidden issues in our communities and states. Beyond a safe place to land, these victims will need clothing, household items, hygiene items, games and toys, or whatever the center needs currently.

We all have too much junk in our basements and closets. Start a new fad, become a minimalist, or at least a less-ist, and donate what you have sitting around that you haven't used in months or years.

Maybe Veteran's issues are your hot button. Seek out a way to help those who have served us so bravely.

Do you find politics interesting? If you feel strongly about issues, your political party has tasks from stuffing letters to making phone calls to showing up at meetings and forums to making a trip to your state capitol during legislative sessions.

Social advocacy your thing? There are groups that support everything from the rights of the LGBTQ community to clean rivers to protecting our elderly. If you feel strongly about it, there's a group out there.

If you look at the items in the list above, most of them cost nothing but time. Obviously as a former fundraiser, I encourage you to give financially to support people and organizations that serve others. But this list only requires your time and interest. It's about being uncomfortable with where you are currently and moving away from your indifference.

You may feel your little contribution of time or money doesn't make a difference. Mother Teresa said this,

> I never look at the masses as my responsibility. I look at the individual. I can only love one person at a time. I can only feed one person at a time. Just one, one, one. . . . The work is only a drop in the ocean. But if I didn't put that drop in, the ocean would be one drop less.

A common proverb in Haiti is, *Men anpil chaypa lou* (Many hands make the load lighter). You can be one of those hands that make the load lighter for people across the table, community, nation, and world.

A few years ago, I wrote a piece on what I learned from Dr. William, from his life as an orphan to doctor. Persevere. Dream big. See the world with new eyes. Give back. These four points apply to the journey of our work in Haiti, a path that took *us* from a nudge to a nonprofit. They likely apply to your journey as well.

## Persevere

An orphan from Haiti has very little chance of success. Many are abused, sold into slavery, or die from lack of food or medical care. William has survived many challenges. He has shown how to persevere against all odds. He taught me to stick with what's worthwhile.

There are times I've truly wanted to walk away from this ministry. Language and cultural differences, along with the distance between here and there, can cause a lack of understanding. Often the real difficulties and requests in Haiti outweigh our ability to care for those needs. Social media is a blessing and a curse. Every day I can keep in touch with people and find out what's going on. But every day I see the pain and often someone asks for something or expects something that I can't deliver.

Recently, we had a misunderstanding with the cost of building in a low area of our Women's Village and ended with a bill that we had no money to pay. I told William that I needed a weekend off, that I wasn't going to respond to anything for one weekend. It allowed me to take a breath, to get some distance from the issue, and realize we'll find a way through.

When we don't have money, persevere. When we can't find a way, persevere. If it's worthwhile, persevere. When I need a weekend off, come back and persevere.

---

A leaking roof may fool the
sun but cannot fool the rain.
*(Yon do kay ki koule ka twonpe
solèy la, men li pa ka twonpe lapli a.)*

---

## See the World through New Eyes

It is wonderful to see our country through William's eyes. He is amazed by how much land we have. Seven countries the size of Haiti could fit in the state of South Dakota. William can't believe how quiet it is here. And he's surprised that we have a machine for everyday tasks—dispensing soda or juice, mowing the yard, washing our dishes, opening the garage door, and so on. On his first trip to the United States, he said to me, "Now I know why people don't want to go back to Haiti." William taught me to look at the world with new eyes.

The wonderful people of LaGonave have helped me to see the world differently. Joy in the midst of extraordinary pain. Generosity in the midst of scarcity. Faith when hope is far off in the distance. Caring for others in the midst of crippling need. Acceptance within all of our differences.

I say often to team members, the board, and myself, "We don't live there. We have to take conscious steps to not impose our will or that we always know a better way."

When people call me boss in Haiti, I say, "Pa boss, ou zanmi." *Not boss, your friend.* I think of my friend Rob. We could have intense arguments but always walked away as friends. Always. We need to walk alongside and support, offer suggestions, and be accepting of a different way. It's only possible when we see the world through their eyes.

---

### The eyes see, the mouth is silent.
### *(Je wè, bouch be.)*

---

## Dream Big

William's sisters said that even as a young boy, William wanted to be a doctor. When our church committed to sponsor William in his medical education, we did so on one condition—that he return to serve the people of Haiti. That was easy for him to agree to since his dream has always been to serve the people on the island of LaGonave. (Dr. William has served as our doctor and ministry leader since 2016).

From the beginning, my goal was just to make a little difference. Even after becoming a nonprofit, my expectations were just do what we can. But I did dream. I dreamt that we could have our own school so we could choose our own teachers, make sure the kids were fed, and have the best educational experience possible. I hoped for a clinic, so we'd have a center where William and nurses, who we've helped with their education, could serve others. The Women's Village is coming to realization with more homes and land than I could have dreamt of in a year of dreams.

I still have projects and hopes for the future. Some might happen, some may not. But as Carl Sandburg says, "Nothing happens unless first we dream."

---

### Hope makes one live.
*(Lespwa fè viv.)*

---

## Give Back

William says all the time, "God watches me, and he always puts someone in my way to help me." William taught me to be that someone in the way. William had an idea to start a Haiti Children's Christmas so kids could get a meal and small toy on Christmas Day. (In 2022, we had over 1,200 kids show up). Someone needs what you and I have to give. God is calling us to give back.

Who will you get in the way of, to help them? What ideas have been rolling round in your mind for far too long and now you're ready to follow that nudge? To whom will you say, "It's my problem and I'm going to be a small part of the solution"?

Over my time in fundraising, I've come to know incredibly generous donors. Some of the most generous are those that give from their heart, making sacrificial gifts. The woman who turned down her heat so she could give more to missions. The wealthy couple who are making plans to give all of their wealth away. The educator who supported the remaining students in our school, because she felt God led her to make a way for these kids. The retired couple who sends monthly $10 checks to support a student. The family that tithed an inheritance and sponsored a house in our Women's Village.

> But a poor widow came and put in two very small copper coins, worth only a few cents. Calling his disciples to him, Jesus said, "Truly I tell you, this poor widow has put more into the treasury than all the others. They all gave out of their wealth; but she, out of her poverty, put in everything—all she had to live on." Mark 12: 42-44 NIV

It's time to persevere, see the world through new eyes, dream big, and give back. However, wherever, whomever—it's time.

---

**God says do your part and I'll do mine.**
*(Bondye do ou. Fe pa ou, M a fe pa M.)*

---

# NEXT STEPS

Leave an Amazon Book Review for this book, *It's Not My Problem . . . Or Is It?*—www.amazon.com.

To find out more about Haiti Alive go to www.HaitiAlive.org.

To support one of our ministries go to www.HaitiAlive.org/donate.

If you have questions or want more information, email the author at contact@HaitiAlive.org.

If you'd like to read Bruce's blog, Parsonage Parables, see his two other books. For further information about the author go to www.BruceBlumer.com.

# APPENDIX A
## *Maps*

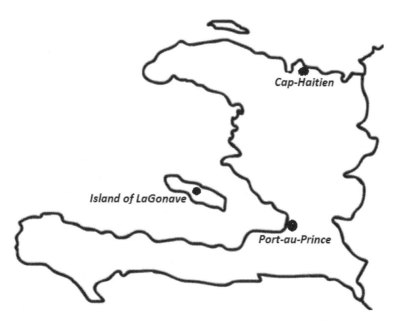

Haiti

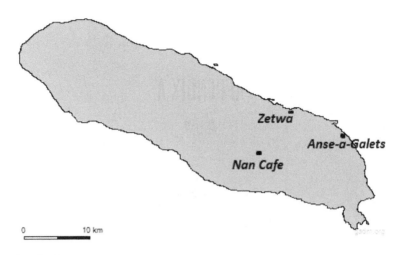

Island of LaGonave

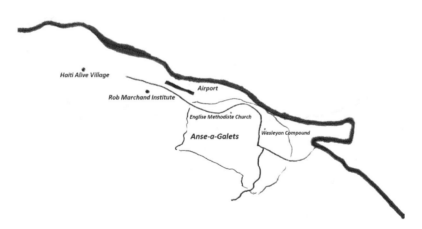

City of Anse-a-Galets

# APPENDIX B
## *Logos*

Original Logo

Current Logo

# APPENDIX C
## *Fundraisers*

### Books by the Author

All Profits Donated to Haiti Alive ($50,000 raised from all publications)

*Paths, Proverbs, & Lessons from Haiti* (2011), reflection and picture booklet

*I Saw God Today* (2013), reflection and picture booklet

*Parsonage Parables* (2015), "the best" of the Parsonage Parables blog

*Even a Little Raindrop* (2017), children's book written in English and Haitian Creole. "Buy a book, give a book" effort distributed 100 books to RMI school children.

*Simply Grace: Everyday Glimpses of God* (2019), GBHEM Publishing

*Turtle Bay* (2020), children's book illustrated by local artist Mardoche Draw and distributed to RMI school children

*Mighty Winds and Gentle Whispers: The Purpose & Power of the Holy Spirit* (2021), GBHEM Publishing

## Fundraising

| | |
|---|---|
| 2011, 2012 | Large Rummage Sales |
| 2016 | "Firm Foundation" fundraiser for RMI School |
| 2018 | "Block by Block" fundraiser, sponsor a block for RMI School |
| 2018 | Buy a square to "Raise the Roof"—number 1–150, the amount you donate, raised about $10,000 / Togetherr developed software to replicate as an online fundraiser ($3,000) |
| 2019 | "10 and Done" fundraiser—ten sections of roof for $1,000, to finish second level of RMI. |
| School Sponsorships | $150/student provides uniform, daily meal, year of education. $100/month to sponsor teachers. |
| Women's Village | $10,000/home, increased to $11,500/home due to material costs. 365 Meters—$55/meter to build a security fence around the village. |

# APPENDIX D
## *Images of Haiti*

Just days after the earthquake; across this quiet bay thousands died or were displaced.

Celebrate Jesus Clinic
(observation deck on
right of the building)

February 2017,
groundbreaking
for Rob Marchand
Institute (RMI)

Foundation of RMI

Construction of RMI

Construction of RMI

September 2018, dedication of RMI

Dedication of RMI. Kate, Mary, Jay Marchand (and new friend).

Second level completed; school bus, 2020

Bruce with RMI Kids; school will be for grades 1-9

Haiti Children Christmas

School supply
giveaway

Elderly food
giveaway

Children feeding program

Original clinic in Zetwa

Annie Zwetzig Clinic

Bruce and Sharon Blumer Clinic

Construction begins for the Women's ~~Clinic~~ Village

Homes provided for women and their families

Building homes provides jobs for local workers

Haiti Alive Village with room for sixty-four homes

Made in the USA
Monee, IL
17 August 2023